the DOUGHNUT KING

the DOUGHNUT KING

JESSIE JANOWITZ

SCHOLASTIC INC.

For Mom and Dad

ISBN 978-1-338-61531-9

12 11 10 9 8 7 6 5 4 3   20 21 22 23 24

Printed in the U.S.A.   40

First Scholastic printing, October 2019

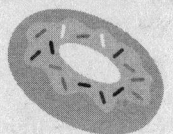

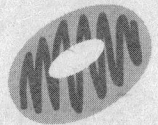

1

Yes!

I couldn't get out of there fast enough. And I wasn't the only one. When that final bell rang, Mrs. Putnam's entire seventh-grade history class rushed to the door like there was free pizza on the other side.

I stopped at my locker on my way out of school to drop off my books. I didn't even want to see them for the next ten days.

Halfway down the hall, I realized I hadn't spun the dial on the lock. Whatever. If somebody were willing to commit a crime for my earth science book, they could have it.

Andy Hubbard, one of the Ice Kings, reached out for a high five as I passed. "Doughnut Boy!"

I tried to slap his hand on the move but ended up giving more

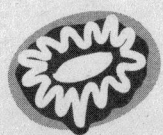

of a high two. "Gotta go!" I called over my shoulder. "Have a good break!"

Since we'd moved upstate midyear, I'd been at Waydin for only three months, but those school days had been the longest of my life. I swear each second of a Waydin day was equal to five minutes of a P.S. 111 day.

It wasn't as if the teachers were any more boring than teachers at my school back in New York City had been. If anything, the teachers at Waydin were better—some were even funny, like Mr. Dodd, who began each class with a Joey Bundano story. Joey was this kid Mr. Dodd grew up with who was always getting into trouble. I'm pretty sure a bunch of the stories were made up—I mean, I don't think one kid could fill his entire apartment with crumpled newspaper in a single night, and definitely not without waking his parents—but who cares? If Mr. Dodd liked to make up stories just to make us laugh, that was fine by me.

The teachers at Waydin weren't the problem. The problem was the kids. There weren't enough of them.

If I'm being honest, this wasn't a problem for everyone. It definitely wasn't a problem for Jeanine, my brainiac, nine-year-old sister. But if you're the kid who has spent every year hiding in the back row, waiting until you got home to figure out in peace and quiet when to use "less" instead of "fewer" or how to find the area of a cylinder, this is a big problem. If you're the kid whose brain turns off when there's an audience, Waydin is your nightmare, because when there are only twelve kids in your whole seventh-grade class, there is no place to hide. There aren't even rows. There's just a circle. And you can see everyone in a circle.

As you've probably guessed, that kid who likes to hide in the back row is me, Tris Levin—or at least it is for another six years until I can legally change my name to Jax. Do you know what it's like to go around every day with a name that just doesn't fit? If you do, the good news is that you can change it. The bad news: you have to wait until you turn eighteen.

Outside, the sky was gray, but kids were lying on the grass using backpacks as pillows like they were at the beach and the sun was shining. Someone was playing music on a phone. It looked like fun, but I didn't have time to lounge around. I had to get to work. And the truth is, I wanted to. Working's different when the whole thing is your idea, especially when that idea is doughnuts— mind-blowing, life-changing, cream-filled doughnuts.

I waited for Jeanine and Zoe in our spot by the side of the building, then together, we walked around back to the parking lot.

Dad was already there.

"It came!" He waved a magazine out of the station wagon's open window. "You made the cover!"

3

What? The Doughnut Stop was on the cover of *Destination Eating*?

Destination Eating is this fancy food and travel magazine for upstate New York, and I was blown away when they called about doing an article on the doughnut business I started with my friend Josh. But just an article. They never said anything about the cover.

I jogged across the parking lot and took the magazine from my father.

There we were: me and Josh, all glossy, knocking doughnuts together, sitting on the ticket counter in the old train station where we opened The Doughnut Stop.

This was huge. People didn't even have to read the magazine to learn about us; they'd just have to see it lying around somewhere. Talk about buzz.

"Let *me* see!" Zoe pulled my hands down. "Why does your face look like that?"

"That's the way his face always looks," Jeanine said, peering at the magazine over Zoe.

"You look so clean and shiny," Zoe said.

"Um, thanks?"

Zoe pulled the magazine lower and sounded out the words under the photo. "'Meet the to-as-t.' To-ast?"

"'Meet the toast of Petersville,'" Jeanine read. "'Two twelve-year-

4

old boys who opened a doughnut shop in the town's abandoned train station.'"

"They don't make toast," Zoe said.

Jeanine rolled her eyes. "It's an expression. They mean a toast like when you knock glasses together and say, 'cheers.'"

"Oh." Zoe sucked her lower lip. She was clearly still confused.

Dad thumped the side of the car. "Come on, guys. Let's go."

We all piled in, me up front, Zoe and Jeanine in back.

I laid the magazine on my knees and then flipped to the article.

There were a couple of photos of me and Josh in the shop selling doughnuts, and then some of me frying them at home. The article took up almost four whole pages.

During the interview, the reporter had asked a bunch of questions about how a banker (Dad) and a chef (Mom) ended up moving their family to a tiny town in upstate New York in the first place, and that's where the article started: *Tris explains that when his father lost his job last fall, his parents decided they wanted a new adventure.*

Just so you know, "adventure" was definitely not the word I used. I don't think I've ever used the word "adventure" unless I was talking about an amusement park.

They packed up and moved from the big city to tiny Petersville, NY, so his mother, a professional chef, could open the town's first restaurant.

When asked to explain where the idea for a cream doughnut shop came from, Tris points to a sign hanging over the counter that reads, "Yes, we do sell chocolate cream doughnuts!"

"That sign was in the window of the General Store my first day in town, but it turned out that the owner, Winnie, didn't make the doughnuts anymore, even though everybody said they were...this sounds weird, but people said they were like...life-changing. Now that I tell the story, it sounds kind of bad, but this all started because I just had to have one of those doughnuts. Then I met Josh and we decided to start the business together, and it really is the best thing I've ever done. I mean, it's not easy, but I still love it."

I closed the magazine and cracked the window. I was starting to feel queasy from reading in the car. I'd finish it later with Josh when he got to The Doughnut Stop after hockey practice.

"So how was school?" Dad asked.

"Fine," Jeanine said. "Oh, except Ms. Shepard doesn't want me helping out after vacation."

Jeanine's math is way beyond what they teach at Waydin, so before we started in January, my parents and the principal agreed that she'd do online courses with the Center for Talented Youth and help out in math classes at Waydin during her free periods.

"But I thought that was going so well," Dad said. "What happened?"

"*I* don't know."

I laughed. "Oh, come on. You correct Ms. Shepard in class in front of everybody."

Dad frowned at the rearview mirror. "You don't. Please, tell me you don't."

"I have an obligation to make sure that the math is correct. That's why Principal Kritcher put me in there."

"Couldn't you at least wait until after class?" Dad said.

"So those kids are supposed to learn it wrong for an entire day?"

I had to admit Jeanine had a point. Dad must have thought so too because he dropped the subject. "How was your day, Zo?"

"Did you know if you suck *really* hard on your arm, you can make a heart?" Zoe pushed up her sleeve and showed us her arm in the rearview mirror.

"You gave yourself a hickey?" I said.

"A heart. It's pretty." Zoe studied her work. "Want one?"

"Uh, no thanks," I said.

"Zo Zo, no hickeys, okay?" Dad said.

"You mean on other people?"

"I mean, on anyone."

"Why?"

"Because… Just don't."

Zoe didn't say anything. I was pretty sure the next chance she had, she'd be spelling her name in hickey.

"And Tris, what about you," Dad said. "Last day before break, how was it?"

"A five."

"School is always a five with you."

"Yeah, well, that's kind of its ceiling."

"That makes me sad."

I hate it when he says that. I mean, I don't want to make him sad, because he's a pretty good dad given the other dads I've seen, and I think he knows that I don't want to make him sad, so is he basically just asking me to lie to him?

"Think of it this way, I never say it's less than a five, right? So that should make you happy."

"But do you ever think maybe, just maybe, it could be a seven? What would that look like?"

"Not school?"

"I give up. Any big plans for spring break?"

"Figure out how to make doughnuts faster."

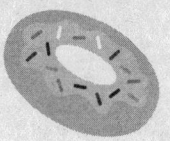

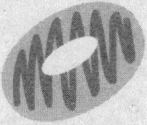

2

We dropped Zoe at home, then headed to town. Jeanine came with me and Dad so she could go to the library, her favorite place on earth.

My favorite place on earth? The NYC Cake and Bake Supply Company.

I had to get to The Doughnut Stop to open at 4:00 p.m. We used to be open just weekends, but in February, Josh and I convinced our parents we could handle Friday hours too. It turns out we can't, but let's just keep that between us.

The doughnuts and cream-filled pastry guns were already in the car. On Fridays, I fry the doughnuts and put them in the car before I go to school. The creams I make the day before, and then Dad just throws them in a cooler on his way out to pick us up.

Mom and I split the old train station: The Doughnut Stop on one

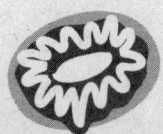

side and The Station House, her restaurant, on the other. When we moved to Petersville, the building was just sitting there, empty, and had been since the train decided it wasn't worth its time to stop there anymore, so Jim, Petersville's mayor, let us use the place rent-free. It's a pretty good deal, especially because Mom does the mom stuff she does at home, like make sure the bathroom is stocked with toilet paper, which is definitely a plus. She doesn't even charge us for it.

Since the station house is on the far end of Main Street with nothing else around, it helps both businesses because we're not out there alone. People who come for the restaurant discover The Doughnut Stop, and the other way around. We've even done some co-branding.

In case you haven't read *Starting Your Own Business for Dummies*, co-branding is where two businesses work together to sell stuff.

Dad takes care of the business side of the restaurant, but the whole thing was Mom's idea, so I always think of it as hers. Hers and Walter's. Walter is Mom's best friend. Before I was born, he and Mom cooked together in restaurants back in the city. When Mom opened The Station House, Walter moved here to run it with her because he and his wife, Azalia, wanted their daughter, Larissa, to grow up in the country like they had back in El Salvador.

It was still cloudy when we got to town, and without some sun, Main Street looked even sadder than usual. Nine small buildings lined the street and half of them were boarded up with FOR SALE signs out front. Maybe they'd started out different colors, but they were all the same peeling gray now. The two exceptions were the library and Dr. Charney's clinic. The library was the only building on Main Street made of brick, and though it wasn't a bright red, at least it was a color. There were also some blue-checked curtains hanging in the windows on the second floor where Josh lived with his mother, the librarian. The clinic was painted Gatorade green with neon-pink trim, and it popped like it was 3-D. Everything else was flat.

Dr. C says colors can actually make us happy and that they make you really happy when they surprise you, so he repaints the clinic every few months—usually in the middle of the night, wearing one of those headlamps miners use. Besides being a doctor, Dr. C is a big-time painter and marathon runner. Before I met him, if someone had told me you could be all those things in one lifetime, I never would have believed them.

Back when we lived in the city, there were six different stores just on my block. When we moved to Petersville, there were just three in the whole town. There was Turnby's, where Harley Turnby sold whatever he felt like for whatever he thought he could get away with, which in Petersville wasn't much. Next to that was the General Store, where Winnie Hammond sold hardware and eggs in colors I didn't know they came in until we moved here, not just white or brown, but green, blue, and something kind of peachy. Across Main Street was Renny's Gas Mart, just a normal gas station and convenience store, which made it kind of unusual for Petersville. And that was it until I opened The Doughnut Stop and Mom opened The Station House.

When Dad and I pulled up in front of the station house that day, the line of customers stretched from the door of The Doughnut Stop, down the porch stairs, and halfway across the parking lot. This wasn't because of the article. It hadn't even hit newsstands yet. We'd just gotten an early copy because we were in it. This was normal, and had been since the FYOs.

Back in December, when Josh and I opened The Doughnut Stop, we'd had only one product: prefilled, chocolate cream doughnuts. But by February, we'd branched out to three other flavors: butterscotch, cinnamon, and vanilla. Then in March, I came up with the idea for the FYO: fill-your-own. Now, just a few weeks later, FYO was all anybody ordered.

I get it. Once you've shot cream into your own doughnut, you'll never go back to prefilled. But you don't have to take my word for it. Come see for yourself.

Selling Tip #31: If you're not gaining a customer, you're losing one. *The Dummies' Guide to Making the Sale.*

By five, I was completely sold out.

I dropped into the armchair in the old ticket booth we use as our office and closed my eyes. I'd been awake for more than twelve hours, and it wasn't even dark yet.

Through the wall separating The Doughnut Stop from The Station House, I could hear Dad singing his moan-y French songs as he checked the pantry shelves. Gone was any hope of catching a nap.

I swiveled around to face the ancient computer and pressed the Power button. The machine groaned to life. It had been a gift from Josh's grandparents when they'd gotten a new one, and it worked fine, so long as you didn't have any plans for the rest of the day.

We keep our to-do list on a clipboard hanging on the wall next to the computer, and I started going through it:

Order napkins—Josh.

RECYCLED ONES!—W

Have you checked the price for recycled? Too expensive—Jeanine

IS THAT WHAT YOU'LL TELL YOUR CHILDREN WHEN THEY ASK YOU WHY THERE ARE NO MORE TREES?—W

Winnie always writes in capital letters. If there were cartoon bubbles floating over our heads with the words we say, Winnie's would be in all caps. And they would smell like cinnamon Tic Tacs.

Winnie Hammond, owner of the General Store, is our business partner for one simple reason: the original chocolate cream doughnut recipe was hers.

We put Jeanine in charge of dealing with our suppliers because even though she's only nine, she likes to yell at people. Plus, she's a math genius, which keeps us from getting ripped off.

Zoe helps out too. She's five, but she's already a decent baker. I know: five seems pretty young for baking, but with my mom, baking ranks even higher than swimming as a life skill. At twelve, I still only doggie paddle, but I make a wicked baked Alaska.

Since Zoe likes to eat as much as she likes to bake, her help wasn't so helpful at first. Then Josh came up with the idea of putting her in his old peewee hockey helmet during her shifts. No way a doughnut fits through the grill on that face guard. Problem solved.

Finally, The Doughnut Stop website popped up on the computer screen. Our site's not fancy or anything, but it gets the job done. Calvin, who works at the Gas Mart, is taking a web design class at Crellin Community College, so he did it just for the experience.

First thing I did was check our emails. Just one from Riley at Stinky Cheese Farm, letting us know when to expect next week's dairy delivery.

Then I clicked on the Comments tab to see what people were saying about us. It was usually the same thing. Stuff like, "These doughnuts are amazing!" I'm not trying to brag, but we've got a good product, and at four in the morning when it's snowing or when the sink is filled with dirty pastry guns, those comments are what get me out of bed or washing up—or whatever it is I should be doing instead of watching cat versus cucumber YouTube videos.

 TheChowingTrucker 20m ago

Somebody told me about this place because I deliver to Albany pretty regular and that takes me by Petersville so I stopped in today. What kind of store doesn't open until 4:00 in the afternoon? Had to wait around in the parking lot like they were selling Bon Jovi tix. Almost left. So glad I didn't. Got to shoot a doughnut full of butterscotch cream—myself! Holy mama! Best doughnut ever. Going back next chance I get.

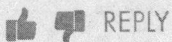 REPLY

I felt my mouth stretch into a smile so big it split my chapped lower lip. *Best doughnut ever.* I knew exactly who this guy was. The Bon Jovi concert T-shirt was a dead giveaway.

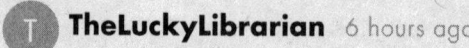 **TheLuckyLibrarian** 6 hours ago

Can't stop eating these doughnuts. You have to try them! Just incredible.

In the interest of full disclosure, my son is one of the owners—the business guy, not the baker. But I'm telling you, even if he weren't, I'd love these doughnuts. And I LOVE getting to choose the cream and filling the doughnut myself. A food AND an activity. Great for kids and adults.

👍 👎 REPLY

Josh's mom. She posts almost the same thing every day. So embarrassing. I mean, super nice, but still embarrassing.

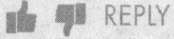 **Anonymous** 4 days ago

DO NOT GO TO THE DOUGHNUT STOP!!!!! THEY DON'T EVEN HAVE DOUGHNUTS. I'VE GONE FOR THE PAST THREE SATURDAYS AND EACH TIME, THEY'VE RUN OUT AND I NEVER GOT ONE. I HEAR THE DOUGHNUTS AREN'T EVEN SO GREAT.

👍 👎 REPLY

I froze.

Do not go to The Doughnut Stop. Those seven words knocked

the wind right out of me, like I'd been flying through the air on a swing, my sneakers touching the trees, and the next second, the ground had reached up and punched me in the face.

Click. Click. Click. How do you delete?

Windows shrunk. Windows multiplied. A new comment box opened. I slammed the mouse onto the counter.

I'd never needed to get rid of a comment before. Josh updated the site. He'd know how, but I didn't want him to see the words, and I didn't want to wait.

I couldn't wait. I had to do it now. Because every second, one more person—maybe more—would see that comment and remember what it said even after I made it disappear.

Click. Click.

It wasn't as if I didn't know we had a supply problem. I just didn't know how to fix it. Yet.

Even with Zoe in the helmet, we couldn't keep up with demand. The major obstacle to increasing doughnut production? The seventh grade. I'm all for education and everything, but do you know how much time is wasted in school? I'm not talking about cutting anything useful, just speeding things up and getting rid of waste, like health class.

Actual health: very important. Waydin Middle School Health Class: useless and completely unrelated to actual health.

Click—

The comment window disappeared.

Ugh!

I got up and paced around waiting for the site to reload.

When the comments were finally back up on the screen, I realized there was one I hadn't read:

 Anonymous 4 days ago

There's a reason we don't let kids run for President. It's the same reason we shouldn't let them run businesses. They're kids! They don't know what they're doing. The Doughnut Stop is run by a kid, and it's a total disaster. I was there last Saturday and that kid was all, "due to high demand, we have a one doughnut per customer limit." Then they ran out anyway. They were supposed to be open for another two hours!! It would have been funny if I hadn't driven almost an hour and really wanted a doughnut.

👍 👎 REPLY

I jumped out of my chair. My insides felt all fizzy, like a soda somebody had shaken up.

I needed to do something.

I climbed over the ticket counter, turned on the sink, and started washing pastry guns.

Squirt. Scrub.

That kid? It had to be me. Josh had been visiting his grandparents last Saturday.

Scrub. Rinse.

Besides, Josh was taller than most adults. And since January, he had shoulders like that guy in the circus who wears leopards around his neck like scarves. Nobody was going to call *him* "that kid."

Squirt. Scrub.

And maybe we *should* let kids run for president! At least kids know when something's not working and say it. And—

"Hey!"

I dropped the pastry gun, which was now cleaner than it had been when I bought it. I turned around.

It was Josh.

"Hey, do you know how to delete comments on our site?"

Josh let his hockey duffel fall to the floor. "Oh, jeez. I forgot. I usually do that, you know, but I was just…" He shook his hair in front of his face. "Did you see, I mean, was there something…" He didn't finish.

But Josh didn't need to finish. The truth was floating right over his head in all caps.

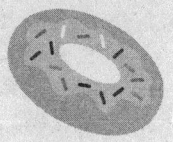
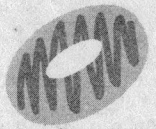

3

"You *knew* we had a problem," Josh said as he kicked his hockey bag behind the counter.

"But I thought we had time to figure it out."

"We did." *Kick.* "We do." *Kick.*

"'Don't go to The Doughnut Stop?' Obviously not!" I shut the water off so hard, the cold knob came off in my hand.

"Why are you mad at *me*? *I* didn't write the stupid comments." He'd turned to face me now but he was still hiding behind his hair.

"Because you lied to me."

"I didn't lie. I…withheld information because I thought sharing it would have a…destructive effect."

I rolled my eyes, cracking a smile against my will.

In addition to being the star of the Petersville Ice Kings, Josh is

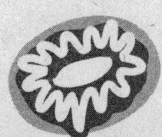

the best English student at Waydin. It's like all those words from all those books on the shelves in the library snuck out in the middle of the night and climbed upstairs into Josh's brain while he was sleeping. He doesn't even remember the names of all the books he's read.

"What if I *had* told you?" he said. "How would knowing about those comments have changed anything?"

"That's not the point." I screwed the knob back into the faucet. "You should have told me."

Josh blew out hard, sending hair flying. "I didn't know what to do. I'm sorry. I just didn't want to..."

"I know," I said, because I did—because the reason he hadn't wanted me to know was the reason he was my best friend in the first place. And now that the shock was wearing off, I could see his point. What good would my knowing have done?

But some part of me just wouldn't let it go. "How many have there been? Total. Like these."

"What does it matter?"

"I just want to know," I said, but I knew why it mattered. For the first time ever, I had a thing: The Doughnut Stop. I even had a nickname, "Doughnut Boy." There was no way I could go back to being plain old Tris.

"Please, just tell me," I said.

"I don't know." Josh's eyes dropped to the floor. "A couple every week?"

"Every week!"

"See, this is why I didn't tell you. It's the internet. People say all kinds of stuff on the internet. According to the internet, dinosaurs helped build the pyramids. It doesn't mean anything."

"But *this* is true! We can't make enough doughnuts, and I have no idea how to make more."

Right then, Dad came bopping through the door smiling ear to ear. You'd think if you'd just spent the last hour counting cans in a closet, you might be a little grouchy, but Dad doesn't do grouchy. If he hadn't become a banker, he'd have made a great kindergarten teacher.

"Ready? If we're going to make it back here for the meeting, we gotta leave now," he said.

"Oh, right." I'd completely forgotten about the town meeting that night. It would be Petersville's first ever. Jim, the mayor, had some big surprise he was unveiling, and it was all anybody had talked about for weeks.

"I'll take out the trash and clean the rest of the guns," Josh said.

"Okay, the ones I haven't done are still in the sink." I went back to the ticket office to get my backpack.

"Wait for you in the car," Dad called.

Josh hurdled over the ticket counter and sat down in front of the computer. "Hey, don't worry about the comments. I'll delete them now." He tapped away at the keyboard.

"Great. Thanks. And if there are any—"

"I swear, from now on, I will tell you every single horrible thing anybody ever says about you or The Doughnut Stop until the end of time. Sound good?" He was smiling under his hair.

"Perfect. I can't wait."

The second Dad turned on the car, *Hello!…Salam!* blared out of the speakers.

"Sorry." He lowered the volume, then waved at me. "*Salam!*"

"Can we please just turn it off?" I needed to think.

"Sorry, got to listen to the whole lesson twice a day."

Good morning! Sabah el kheer! The woman sounded like a cheerful robot.

"*Sabah el kheer!*" Dad repeated, imitating not just the accent but all her cheerful robot-ness too.

When Dad's not working on restaurant stuff, he's teaching himself Arabic—or at least, that's what he's doing this month. Last month, he was watching YouTube videos to learn how to tap the trees around our house so we could make our own maple syrup. That was until Jeanine figured out that the trees he thought were maples were actually sycamores. Turns out, we don't have any maple trees. Ever heard of sycamore syrup? Yeah, there's a good reason for that.

Thank you. Shukran.

"*Shukran. SHUkran? ShuKRAN?*" Dad's eyebrows waggled as he tried out the word.

Every second of this car ride was going to be painful, but I would never forget my earphones ever again.

"I found it!" Jeanine shook a bunch of papers in Dad's face as she slid into the back of the station wagon.

How are you?...Kayf halik?

"Hold on a sec." Dad turned off the stereo.

I shot him a look.

"What? *You* just didn't want to listen to it. *She's* actually going to talk to me."

"I'm applying for the Young Leaders of America Scholarship!" Jeanine announced like this was exciting news for the entire universe.

"That's great!" Dad said. "What is it?"

"One week in D.C. to see how government really works. *And* you get to go to the White House and meet with different members of Congress." Jeanine's head bounced up and down in the rearview mirror. "Isn't that amazing?"

"Amazing." Dad nodded. Both my parents do a lot of nodding when Jeanine is talking.

"I know, *and* we get a special tour of the White House. Not the one just everybody can get. *We* get to go into the Oval Office."

"What do you have to do to win?" I asked.

"Just write a really good essay about how I'm a leader in the community. You're supposed to explain how you're making a difference. I can do that. No problem. I'm a killer essay writer."

"Isn't what they really care about what you're doing, not how good a writer you are?" I said.

"The application says the people with the best essays will be selected, which means they want the best writers."

"I'm not sure that's entirely right, Jeannie," Dad said in the same careful way he tells Zoe that Henry, her rabbit, probably won't learn to say, "Henry wants a carrot," no matter how many times he hears her say it.

I turned around to face Jeanine. "Yeah, I mean, if they want to know how you're making a difference, don't you think they're judging people on that?"

"How would *you* know? How many scholarships have *you* won?"

"Jeanine," Dad warned.

Just so you know, it doesn't bother me that I could never win those Solve-a-Thons or Geography Bees like Jeanine does. What bothers me is that my parents think they need to protect me from hearing Jeanine say that I couldn't like it's some big secret.

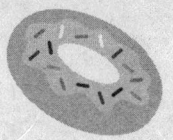

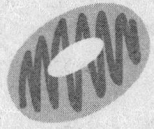

4

Jim's truck was there when we pulled up in front of the house. In addition to being the mayor, Jim's the fix-it guy, and since our house is always in need of fixing, he's over a lot—sometimes to fix the thing he just fixed. This isn't because he can't do it right the first time, but because what we really need is an exorcist. That's the person you call when something is controlled by an evil spirit—I googled it.

Just so you know, I don't believe in witches or ghosts or monsters under my bed, but I'd swear on my KitchenAid mixer that our house has a mind of its own and likes to mess with us. It's also the color of grape juice and looks like was built by a fifth-grade shop class.

I call it the Purple Demon.

My parents do not believe in the Purple Demon, even though

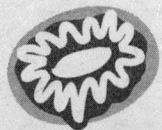

no electrician, plumber, or fix-it person can tell them why all the lights go out several times a month or why the downstairs toilet always does a triple flush, flooding the bathroom.

As soon as Dad stopped the car, Jeanine jumped out. "How much time do we have before the meeting?"

"We'll leave in about an hour," Dad said.

She gave a thumbs-up and took off across the lawn.

"What's the rush? You're on break!" Dad called after her. My parents are always trying to get Jeanine to study less and spend more time outside.

"I need to Skype Kevin about the scholarship!" she called back without stopping.

Kevin Metz has been Jeanine's best friend since they met in Gifted and Talented in kindergarten, and somehow they're still JeanineandKevin even though we live in Petersville now.

"We're home!" Dad called, as we came through the door.

"Hi!" Mom shouted from the kitchen.

Dad hung up his jacket and headed for the stairs. "I'm grabbing a quick shower before the meeting!"

"Good, I can smell you from here!"

"Very funny!"

"Shhhhh!" Zoe's hand waved over the back of the living room couch.

"'Hello' to you too," Dad said as he jogged up the stairs.

"Five! Four! Three! Two! One! AAAAAANNN!" Zoe shouted at the television.

My parents think TV rots your brain unless you're watching a show that teaches you how to cook something. Basically, they'll let us watch anything if it has to do with food. I've tried telling them that there are plenty of educational channels we could watch, like the History Channel or Discovery, but they said I could read about all that other stuff—which doesn't really make sense, because I could read a cookbook too. I think they just didn't want to change the rule. In our house, once a rule is made, my parents stick to it even when it stops making sense—or, in this case, never made sense. I think someone must have told them that to be good parents, you can't rethink your own rules.

So cooking shows are what you get at my house, and before you knock them, you should know that you can learn some pretty handy tricks from watching those shows. Did you know if you smash a garlic clove with a can, the peel basically pops off?

The thing is, in most cooking shows, there's no story: no aliens take over the planet, no twins switch places, no kids hack the school computer—people just cook. Unless you're dying to learn how to make a chocolate soufflé, it gets boring fast. That's why we started watching *Can You Cut It?*. It's a kids' cooking contest, but unlike regular cooking shows, there are bad guys and heroes, winners and losers. If you're lucky, you even get to see blood or tears or both.

I dropped my backpack and sat down on the couch next to Zoe. She had on her Chef JJ bald cap. She must have put it on by herself because her orange hair puffed out all around the bottom like a clown collar. "Does this mean bald people don't scare you anymore?"

"Chef JJ's not bald. She didn't *lose* her hair. She *shaved* it. It's different."

"Nice tattoo," I said.

"Mom did it for me," she said, admiring the NEVER GIVE UP on her bicep. "When I get mine for real, it's going to be purple bubble letters."

"You're getting a tattoo?"

"Mommy said, 'We'll see.'"

"Do you know how you get a tattoo? It's like, really, really painful. They put the ink into your skin with needles."

"Nah-unh."

"Yuh-huh. How do think they get it on so it doesn't come off?"

"I don't care." She stood up on the couch and began to jump. "We're tough."

"We?"

"Me." *Bounce.* "And Larissa. She's getting one too."

"If you say so." Last time Zoe got blood taken, both my parents had to hold her down while she screamed, "Child abuse!"

"Shhhhh!" Zoe landed on her butt on the couch, her eyes glued to the TV. A boy's face, bottom lip trembling, filled the screen. "Bet you a dollar Jackson cries."

"Zo, you scare me sometimes."

"It's just TV."

"You know these are real kids, right?"

Zoe shrugged.

"I thought we were rooting for Jackson." I'd watched Jackson win One Ingredient Masterpiece with this amazing chickpea popcorn creation, but I'd missed the last two episodes.

"We're for Lily now. She can chop three onions in seventy-two seconds. She won Knife Skills Showdown *and* Blind Cooking Challenge. Plus she's a ridmick gymnast."

"A what?"

She waved her arms around. "With the ribbons, remember?"

"Oh, right."

The Olympics is an exception to the nothing-but-cooking-shows rule—don't ask, it doesn't make sense—and somehow whenever we turned it on last summer, rhythmic gymnastics was all we could find.

Did you know there are individual *and* team events in rhythmic gymnastics?

Zoe and I watched as Jackson mashed his lips together to stop them quivering. I should have taken Zoe's bet. Jackson looked like he was going to hold it together, which couldn't be easy with Chef JJ lasering him with her neon-blue eyes. Chef JJ must wear colored contacts. That, or she's an alien.

Next to her, Dieter, co-host of *Can You Cut It?* bent over to study the steak Jackson had made.

Dieter Koons, food critic and restaurant owner, wears three-piece suits in different shades of green and glasses that look like the ones they give out free at 3D movies. I'm pretty sure he's only on the show because they need someone to talk while Chef JJ tastes, chews, and thinks, which would be an okay amount of quiet time in real life but not on national television.

Chef JJ scratched the stubble of her shaved head so hard, her microphone picked up the *scritch scritch*. She looked as disappointed as Zoe that Jackson wasn't bawling.

Mom actually worked with JJ Jordan right out of cooking school—that's why we started watching the show in the first place—and she says Chef JJ was making people cry even back then.

"What. Color. Is. That?" Chef JJ stabbed a slice of meat with a gleaming steak knife.

"Pink?" Jackson's voice caught, breaking the word in two.

"And is that rare, Jackson?"

"But I had to keep—"

Chef JJ put her bony hand up like a stop sign, and Jackson's face went the color his beef should have been.

"Oh, Jackson," Dieter said. "You did a mistake. Do you know what was it?"

Zoe's hand shot in the air. "*Ooo*, I know! I know!"

"'*Made* a mistake.' '*Made* a mistake,'" Chef JJ snapped. "Not '*did* a mistake.' How many times do I have to tell you?"

"What was Jackson's mistake?" I asked Zoe when the show broke for ads.

"He thought rare was *here*." She pressed her middle finger and the tip of her thumb together.

In case you get to watch something other than cooking shows, Zoe was talking about the finger test. The finger test is how you tell meat doneness just by feeling it. Rare meat should feel like the gushy part of your palm when you're making the okay sign. You could just cut into the meat or use a meat thermometer, but that's rookie and would never fly on *Can You Cut It?*

At the end of the commercial break, there was a clip of Chef JJ in front of the Food Connection building in Manhattan talking directly to the camera. "Want to know if you can cut it? Come find out. We're looking for chefs ages eight to fourteen for next season. Go to canyoucutit.com for details on sending an audition video."

"*I* could cut it," Zoe said.

"You so could, but you're going to have to wait a couple years." Zoe versus Chef JJ would be like the World Cup of *Can You Cut It?*

"And I'd wear a shirt for The Doughnut Stop just like Gus did for The Empanada Factory." Gus won last season and he plugged his parents' empanada chain every chance he got.

I kicked off my shoes and settled back to watch the rest of the show.

"*Uch!*" I jerked my hand back from the seat cushion. There was a brown smear across it and a matching one on the sofa.

"Zoe!" I showed her my hand.

"Sorry, Henry's potty training. Don't worry. I put him in time out."

"But you left his poop on the couch?"

"I'll clean it later."

"Clean it now." I shoved her off the couch with my clean hand.

"But—"

"Go! Or I'll tell Mom Henry was on the couch."

"Like *you* never had an accident," she yelled as she ran out of the room.

When I came back from washing my hands, Lily was on the

screen talking about what she'd do with the $100,000 prize money if she won. She had a fancy houseboat picked out already, and she was telling Chef JJ all about it, but I wasn't paying attention anymore. I was thinking, if *I* had all that money, could I solve our doughnut supply problem?

I'd still have to go to school. There's a lot you can do with $100,000, but you can't add hours to the day or change the law requiring kids to go to school.

And even if we could afford to hire people and teach them to make doughnuts, where would we put them? It's not as if my parents were going to give up our kitchen entirely to doughnut-making, and there wasn't enough room in Josh's kitchen. In New York City, Mom would rent a commercial kitchen when she had a big catering job, but that wasn't an option in Petersville.

Even with $100,000, I had no clue how to solve our supply problem.

The Doughnut Stop was in serious trouble.

Jackson was on the screen now, explaining about how he'd use the prize money to start a *pho* place, one of those Vietnamese restaurants where you choose the ingredients and they cook them into a soup right in front of you. Fast-food *pho*.

I stood up. I had to get out of there, away from Jackson, because even though he didn't know the rules for testing meat doneness, he was full of ideas, which made me feel even worse for not having any of my own.

Mom was flipping through a cookbook when I walked into the kitchen.

"Where's Jim?" I asked.

She waved in the direction of the basement door.

"The noise back?"

"I don't want to talk about it."

For the past few weeks, every couple of days, it sounded like a motorcycle was revving its engine in the basement, but as soon as someone got to the bottom of the stairs, it would stop. The Purple Demon likes to change things up.

"Oh, hey!" Mom looked up. "I saw the magazine. The cover! So amazing."

"Yeah."

She studied my face. "What's wrong?"

"Nothing." My parents already thought I took The Doughnut Stop too seriously. It didn't help that during the failed more-doughnuts-less-sleep experiment, I'd passed out in history, sliced my chin open, and ended up needing stitches and a tetanus shot.

It wasn't the doughnuts' fault that a screw was sticking out of my desk, but they blamed them anyway.

The basement door swung open, and Jim appeared, his brown hair and beard gray with soot.

Mom jumped up. "So?"

"It's not the boiler. Turned it off. Took it apart. Put it back together. There's nothing in there that would cause that kind of noise."

"What about the generator?"

Just then, we heard Zoe shout, "You can't cut it!"

"Okay, Zo Zo!" Mom called. "Turn it off now!"

"I didn't check the generator, but I can't now." Jim untied a sweatshirt from around his waist. "I'll come back tomorrow."

Mom grabbed a sweatshirt sleeve. "Please, I'm begging you. Check the generator before you go. I'll whip up those hazelnut scones you love so much."

"Well, now you're not playing fair, but I can't, not even for hazelnut scones. I've got to get ready for the meeting."

"Oh, fine." Mom let go of the sweatshirt.

"Almost forgot. Can you sell coffee and tea tonight?"

"I *could*…if you tell us what the surprise is. Tell me it's a farmers' market." Mom crossed her fingers on both hands.

"It's not a farmer's market," Zoe said, skipping into the kitchen with Jeanine trailing behind her. "It's a big kid playground with a swirly slide."

"No way," Jeanine said. "Swirly slides are responsible for more injuries than any other piece of playground equipment."

"But I *love* swirly slides," Zoe said.

"I do too," Jim said.

"See!" Zoe stuck her tongue out at Jeanine. "We're getting a swirly slide. We're getting a swirly slide," she sang.

"Sorry. No farmers' markets or swirly slides," Jim said.

"You're…you're mean," Zoe said and ran out of the room before Mom could get her to take it back.

"Don't expect Mom to make coffee now that she's not getting a farmers' market," I said.

"No, there'll be coffee," Mom said. "Walter's up there already making some. We're even doing snacks. But I want to know what's wrong with a farmers' market."

"Nothing," he said. "It's a good idea. And I'm not saying we're not going to do it, but that's not what the meeting's about."

"Is it better than a farmers' market and maybe colder?" Josh and I, and just about everybody else in Petersville, were wishing the town surprise was a place to skate that we didn't have to shovel when it snowed. We didn't even need an indoor rink since there's one in Crellin, just something covered. Ice hockey is huge in Petersville, probably because winters here go on forever.

"It's not better than a farmers' market or an ice rink or a swirly slide. It's not better than anything." Jim lowered himself into a chair as if he suddenly remembered he was too tired to stand.

"Jim?" Mom said.

He tugged on his beard. "See, it's not better than anything because it's not something good."

"Then you really shouldn't have called it a surprise," Jeanine said.

Mom narrowed her eyes at Jeanine, and Jeanine gave her a "What?" look.

"I needed people to be there, and I didn't want to worry anybody," Jim said.

"So it's a bad surprise?" I said.

"Oh, yeah," he said slowly as he rocked back and forth in a full-body nod. "Town's disappearing."

Just then my father called from upstairs, "Guys! We should go."

Jim looked at his watch and stood up. "Shoot. I'm going to be late to my own meeting. Now that's just not professional."

And then he was out the door before we could ask him how a town could disappear.

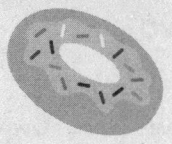
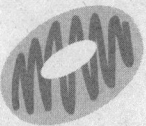

5

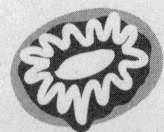

"*Places* don't disappear," Jeanine said as we drove to the meeting. "It's impossible."

"What's a duck's favorite time of day?" Zoe asked.

Jeanine groaned.

"Somebody say 'what,'" Zoe said.

"What?" I said.

"The quack of dawn! Get it?"

"I'm just saying, a place is a place forever," Jeanine said to her own reflection in the car window. "It doesn't go away." She sounded just as sure as she always does, but if she'd been trying to convince someone besides herself, I'm pretty sure she would have been facing the other way.

"Oh, I just thought of one," I said. "What's a duck's favorite candy?"

"What?" Zoe said.

"Quacker Jacks."

"What are Quacker Jacks?" Zoe said.

"Come on, you've never had Cracker Jacks? The popcorn with the—"

"You know"—Zoe patted my arm—"the Laugh Doctor says if you have to explain a joke, it's not funny." *The Laugh Doctor* is a kid's guide to writing and telling jokes, and Zoe's had it read to her so many times, she knows it by heart.

"Of course places don't disappear." Mom was staring out her window too, even though there was nothing to see but black mountains and black fields and black sky that all just blended together in the dark.

"He didn't mean like *poof* disappear," I said.

"So what *did* he mean?" Jeanine asked.

"Let's just wait and hear Jim say what he meant," Mom said.

"Maybe it's a trick. Like when Uncle Philippe makes the penny disappear and then it comes out your ear," Zoe said.

"You think Jim's going to pull Petersville out of your ear?" I tugged on Zoe's earlobe.

Sometimes making Zoe laugh makes me feel better, like that time we got stuck in an elevator, and I pretended I thought it was really funny even though I was scared nobody would figure out we were in there, and I'd have to climb out the top and up the cables like they do in movies. Just a tip: if you ever get stuck in an elevator, look for an emergency phone before you think about pulling a *Mission Impossible*. We'd been in there for an hour before I saw the button.

"Uncle Philippe doesn't make the penny disappear, nuddy," Jeanine said. "He's hiding it between his fingers."

Mom spun around in her seat. "Jeanine, what did I say about calling her 'nuddy'?"

Nuddy's short for *nudnik*, which means stupid in a language my great-grandparents spoke and pretty much nobody speaks anymore. Mom uses it sometimes, but we're not allowed. Don't ask how come she can use it and we can't. It's another one of those rules that doesn't make any sense, and we basically ignore it.

"Is that true, Mommy?"

"I think we just need to wait and see what happens at the meeting," Mom said.

"No, about Uncle Philippe and the penny?"

"Oh, um, I don't know."

"She knows," Jeanine whispered.

"Jeanine!" Dad gave her his squinty "Watch it" look in the rearview mirror.

Jeanine shot a "What?" look back. "If I ever have kids, I'm going to tell them the truth about everything from the beginning."

"Good luck with that," Mom said.

"Maybe you guys misheard Jim," Dad said, taking a hand off the steering wheel and putting it over Mom's.

"I don't think so, honey." She was still staring at her window.

"I'm just saying, it's possible," he said. "Like remember when I thought the school nurse said Zo Zo had a bee up her nose, and it turned out it was a bead."

"But weren't you on your cell?" I said. "We were right there in the room with Jim. Besides, what else could he have been saying?"

It was quiet for a bit, then Dad said, "'The town's in a clearing' kind of sounds like, 'The town's disappearing.'"

"Uh, maybe, but it makes no sense," I said.

Dad thumped the steering wheel. "Wait! I've got it. 'I'm losing my hearing!' That's it! Jim's losing his hearing so he's stepping down as mayor. See, that *does* make sense. And that *would be* a bad surprise." He grinned at me in the rearview mirror.

Just so you know, Dad's not a nuddy. He knew we'd heard what we'd heard. He was just trying to do with all of us what I'd tried with Zoe, but I'm not five. I know what I heard, and whatever it meant, I knew it was bad.

Wham! The smell of toasting corn and frying pork hit me the second I opened The Station House door.

"Pupusas!" Zoe shouted and took off to the back of the restaurant where people were packed around the counter.

"Surprise!" Mom said. "Walter and Azalia made them as a 'thank-you' to everyone for helping them get settled."

In case you've never had them, pupusas are like silver dollar pancakes, but they're made out of corn flour and stuffed with pork or beans or cheese. They're like breakfast, lunch, and dinner all rolled into one, and Walter has been making them for us since we had teeth.

All the tables were pushed to the sides of the room, and the chairs were lined up in rows in the center. Nobody was sitting yet though. Almost everyone was standing at the counter either waiting for a pupusa or eating one. You could tell who was on line for seconds by their greasy smiles.

"Right foot, yellow!" someone called out.

I turned around, and there, in a corner by the door, was a Twister mat spread on the floor with Dr. C, Josh, and Cal, the kid who works at the Gas Mart, all tangled up across it. Josh's arms and legs looked almost braided together, and his face was pressed to his knees.

"Hands on the mat at all times!" Harley Turnby called. Harley was balanced on a folding chair—he was too wide for all of him to fit on it—a Twister spinner propped on one watermelon-shaped knee and a paper plate on the other. "You're up, Dr. C." Harley took an enormous bite of pupusa and flicked the spinner with his thumb. "Left foot, red!" he called, bits of pupusa raining down on the spinner.

"Left foot, red. Left foot, red." From a tabletop position, Dr. C straightened a leg and wove it between the arms of the kid from the Gas Mart. "Got it!" he said, touching the toe of a paint-splattered sock to the edge of a red circle.

Cal turned his pimply face away from Dr. C's bare, hairy thigh. "There should really be a rule about wearing pants for Twister."

"Sorry, squeezed in a run after my last patient."

"Man," Calvin said, stretching out the *a*. "And you didn't shower? Shouldn't doctors be clean freaks?"

"Actually, most people wash too much. See, bacteria—"

"Would you please spin?" Josh begged. His legs were shaking.

"Hold your horses!" Harley took another bite of pupusa, sucked his fingertips, and gave the arrow a flick.

"I told him not to bring that thing," someone said behind me. I'd have known who it was even if I hadn't heard her rattling the Tic Tacs.

I turned to find Winnie, head back, pouring Tic Tacs into her mouth.

"What's wrong with Twister?" I asked. "He thought it'd be fun."

"Fun." Winnie rolled her eyes, then whipped her yellow-white braid over her shoulder and waved me in close like she had a secret to tell.

Her breath was so cinnamon-y, my nose burned when I inhaled.

"Wake up, Slick. Harley Turnby doesn't care about people having fun. This is marketing, pure and simple. Some toy store in Albany was going out of business. He bought a carload full of Twisters for nothing. See?" She pointed to a stack of the games under Harley's chair. "The man is selling, which brings me to my question for you: Why aren't we? How come The Doughnut Stop's not open? Look at all these people shoving their faces. Why aren't they shoving them with doughnuts?"

I should have seen this coming. "We sold out."

"So!" she spat.

"So, we can't sell doughnuts we don't have, right?"

"Don't get smart with me, Slick. I meant, so what are we doing? We can't grow the business if we keep selling out."

"I know. I know!"

"Well, ex*cuse* me. If you *know* what the problem is, then fix it."

"I'm working on it."

"Oh, yeah, how?" Winnie saw right through me.

"I'm thinking about it, okay?"

"Well, think faster."

"Thanks. That's helpful."

"Anytime," she said and shook some more Tic Tacs into her mouth.

A few minutes later, Jim climbed on a chair and yelled for everybody to sit.

Eventually everyone did, but they were still chatting, and Jim's "quiet downs" weren't making any difference. Then Walter clanged two pans together, and the room went silent.

"So when are we getting the rink?" someone called from the back of the room. People cheered. I turned around.

Andy Hubbard, Josh, and the other Ice Kings lined the back wall and were giving each other high fives.

This was not going to go well. Jim had better have a plan for a quick getaway.

"We'll get to the…surprise soon." Jim pulled a crumpled sheet of paper from his pocket and smoothed it on his chest. "But before we get to that, I just wanted to say, this is the first ever Petersville town meeting, as most of you know because, well, you've never been to one before, but I just thought I should say it because a first ever anything is a big deal, right?"

"If he's going to be making these meetings a regular thing, he should really consider public speaking classes," Jeanine said.

"Ice rink. Ice rink…" the Ice Kings began to chant.

Jim tried to quiet them down but it was no use.

Walter looked like he was about to bang the pans again when Jim climbed onto the counter and shouted, "The post office is closing!"

That did it. The room went so quiet I could hear the whine of Mr. Skinner's hearing aid all the way in the front row.

"Weird," Dad said. "That doesn't sound at all like, 'The town is disappearing.'"

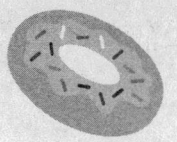
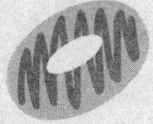

6

At first, I didn't get it either. How big a deal could it be that the post office was closing? How often had I even been to a post office in my life?

I had to be missing something. I knew that from the look on Jim's face, the same weighted-down one he'd had that afternoon in our kitchen.

"Big deal?" Harley Turnby called. "We can just go to Crellin."

"We want to know the surprise!" somebody shouted.

A bunch of people "yeah-ed."

"We want the rink. We want the rink..." the Ice Kings sang.

"Don't you get it?" Jim shouted over them. He was shaking his head and tugging on his beard. This "annoyed" Jim was at least better than the "crushed" Jim from earlier. "You don't get an ice rink! If you don't get a post office, you're not getting an ice rink!"

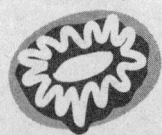

The room went quiet.

"So what *do* we get?" Cal said.

"Nothing!" The parts of Jim's face that hadn't been taken over by beard were nearly purple.

"And *that's* the surprise?" Cal said.

"That's right."

"But that's not a surprise." Harley wagged a finger at Jim.

"They're right," Jeanine said. "He never should have called it a surprise. That was a mistake."

"Jeannie, remember what we said about only saying the helpful things," Mom said.

"You want a surprise?" Jim yelled. "Ready? Here it is: Petersville is disappearing. Surprise! We're going to be like the Roman Empire or Atlantis or Troy. Just like that. One day, Petersville won't be here anymore. The place most of us have lived our whole lives and the place our parents lived their whole lives and their parents lived their whole lives. Not today or tomorrow, but I'm telling you, if we don't do something fast, Petersville will disappear like the dinosaurs." Then he threw his head back and cackled. His eyes were bulging and his beard was sticking out in all directions.

"What's wrong with Jim?" Jeanine asked.

"He's okay. Just a little...overwhelmed," Mom said.

"See? He *should* take a public speaking class."

"Jeanine," Mom said through her teeth.

"What? That's helpful."

Up front, Walter had brought Jim a glass of water, and he was guzzling it down. When the cup was empty, he handed it back with a "thank you," and exhaled like he was blowing out candles on a birthday cake.

"You want to sit down, Jim?" Dr. C called.

Jim shook his head. "Anybody want to guess how many people have moved to Petersville in the last five years? Come on. Give me a number."

Zoe shouted out, "Three million and four and three hundred and twenty."

"Eight," Jim said. "The Levins, that's five. And the Ramirezes, that's three."

"So?" Cal shouted.

"Yeah, is that really so bad?" Harley asked.

"It is when you consider that sixty-four have moved away in the same period."

"Why?" Josh asked. "I mean, we can survive without a post office."

"How about a school? Can Petersville survive if Waydin closes? Schools that weren't even as small as Waydin have closed all over upstate New York. Basically, what we're hearing is that it doesn't make sense for the State to pay to keep open a school for so few students."

I knew small classes were bad news for me, but I'd never thought they might be bad news for the whole town.

"If Waydin closes, kids will have to travel a full hour to the school in Crellin, which will mean families moving away to be closer to the school. And if there are fewer people living here, what will happen to the businesses over time? To Turnby's? To the Gas Mart? How will The Station House stay open if it doesn't have local customers?"

"But the restaurant is doing well, right, Mom? Really well, right?" Jeanine asked.

"Shhh," Mom whispered, without looking at her. "Let's just listen."

"But, Mom?" Jeanine said.

Dad put his arm around Jeanine. "Of course. It's doing great."

"But if it weren't, we'd get to move back to the city, right?" Jeanine asked.

"But it *is* doing great," Dad said.

"But *if* it weren't, we'd get to move back, right?"

"But it *is* doing great," Dad repeated.

Jeanine may be the one with the genius IQ, but she still thinks we could move back to the city whenever my family wanted. *I* once had so many spelling mistakes on a history paper, the teacher asked my parents if English was my second language. *I'm* not the genius, but I know we moved to Petersville because my father lost his job.

Nobody told me. I just knew. I never believed we moved here only because my parents wanted "something different," no matter how many times they said it, just like I didn't believe them then that The Station House was doing "great."

"This isn't about the post office," Jim said. "It's about what the closing of the post office *means* about the future of Petersville."

Mr. Jennings, who owns a turkey farm a few miles from our house, stood up. "So what are we going to do?"

"Exactly!" Jim snapped and pointed at Mr. Jennings. "*What* are we going to do?"

"Uh, yeah, that's what I said." Mr. Jennings looked around the room to see if others were as confused as he was.

"*What. Are. We. Going. To. Do?*" Jim was shouting now.

"I think Jim's having some kind of breakdown," Jeanine said.

"Are we going to lie down and let Petersville disappear?" Jim called like he was a cheerleader at a pep rally.

The room was silent. Maybe pompoms would have helped.

"*No!* Come on, folks; no, we're not. Say it with me."

"No," some of us said like we were in first-period health class: *Do we have potato chips for breakfast? Uh, no?*

"Do we want to be like the dinosaurs?" Jim shouted.

"Yes! The flying kind," Zoe yelled.

"No!" Jim yelled back. "We're going to fight!"

57

A second later, the song from that old boxing movie my Grandma Esme loves was pouring out of the speakers, and someone shadowboxed out of the stockroom in a ladies' bathrobe and red boxing gloves. You couldn't see his face behind the gloves, but whoever it was had very white, very skinny arms and legs.

Jim took the boxer's arm and threw it in the air like the guy was a prizefighter, only now we could see he wasn't. He was Riley Carter, our dairy guy, though it did take me a second to recognize him without his Stinky Cheese Farm baseball cap.

Jim pumped Riley's fist in the air. "Petersville, we are going to fight, and we will survive! Want to know how?"

People mumbled to each other.

Jim dropped Riley's arm. "I said, 'Do you want to know how?'"

Some peopled "yeah-ed." Others "okay-ed." Nobody really seemed all that interested, but I guess it was good enough because that's when Jim said, "Okay, Riley, show 'em!"

Riley threw off the robe and let it fall to the floor. Underneath, he wore shiny, white shorts and a white T-shirt that read in big black letters: PETERSVILLE, THE PLACE TO EAT.

Jim reached behind his back, pulled a magazine from his jeans pocket, unrolled it, and held it up high. "*This* is how we're going to survive."

"What is it?" Mr. Jennings said.

"Our future." Jim winked.

"Uh, okay. But really?" Mr. Jennings said.

"It's *Destination Eating's Guide to the Best Small Towns in America*," Riley said.

"Was this Stinky Cheese's idea?" Harley asked.

"You be quiet," Jim said. "This *was* Riley's idea, and it's a darn good one. Petersville is going to become one of the best small towns in America."

"Oh, yeah," Winnie said. "How?"

Riley knocked his gloved hands together. "Food! Food is *in*! Like, *in* in. I'm talking big-time. And like, fresh stuff—everything homemade from real, whole ingredients, like my cheese and Mr. Jennings's turkey, and what The Doughnut Stop and The Station House sell. Food is like, majorly big right now, and people will travel and spend all kinds of money for a super-special food experience."

"A food *experience*?" Renny said. "You mean eating. Eating is just eating." This wasn't surprising coming from a man who sells Hostess cupcakes that are older than I am.

"Eating is just eating? Renny, man, that makes me sad." Riley put a boxing glove over his heart. "I'm coming to the Gas Mart tomorrow with my Ooey Gooey Camembert. You experience that stinky perfection and then tell me that eating is just eating."

"Can someone tell me why this boy thinks stinky is something that you want from your food?" Renny asked.

"Let me break it down," Jim said. "People eat food. People want good food. We have good food. People come here to eat and buy food. We get money. Some people like it here so much, they move here. Petersville survives. The end."

Now I got it.

Jim was going to bring people to town on the promise of doughnuts I didn't have, the doughnuts I couldn't make enough of, for the people who were coming now.

Going back to "plain old Tris" was one thing. Becoming the kid who let Petersville go extinct was another. Our doughnut supply problem had just gone from serious to epic.

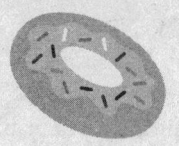
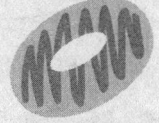

7

Jim spent the rest of the meeting explaining his "Main Street Makeover" plan.

Step one: give Main Street a facelift. We were all supposed to sign up at the library to help clean out, repair, and paint all the storefronts.

Step two: open new stores. Jim was holding a contest for the best new shop ideas. The winners would get to rent the empty buildings for a dollar a month.

The meeting ended when a fight broke out between two women who both wanted to start a quilting shop. At least a quilting store sold stuff people might actually buy. Mr. Jennings wanted to open a shop that would sell the old animal bones he'd collected on his property over the years, some of which he'd made into lamps.

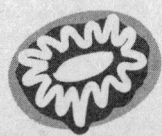

The second we got into the car, Jeanine started blabbing about how Jim's plan was never going to work if we didn't get the word out about Petersville. She thought the *Destination Eating* article on The Doughnut Stop would help, but it wouldn't be enough. "We need something huge. Like, TV commercial huge."

"Commercials are really expensive," Dad said.

"I know. That's why I said '*like* a TV commercial.'" Jeanine rolled her eyes.

Zoe tugged on Jeanine's sweatshirt. "When I'm old enough, I'm going on *Can You Cut It?*"

Jeanine was suddenly bouncing up and down. "That's it! It's perfect!"

"I know!" Zoe said, bouncing too.

"Not *you*. Tris."

I laughed. "Forget it, Jeanine."

"*See*, he doesn't even want to go," Zoe said.

"That show was like, made for you. How can you not even want to try?"

"Because I have The Doughnut Stop."

That was true, but it wasn't the only reason. It wasn't why I didn't even need to think about it. It wasn't why I'd never thought about sending an audition tape to *Can You Cut It?* It wasn't the cooking. It was all the other stuff, the competing with everyone watching. I'd competed before in basketball and soccer, but always on a team. This was all on your own. This was like having to do a math problem in your head in front of the whole class, only instead of a whole class, it would be the whole television-watching world.

"Think about it," Jeanine said. "You could talk all about The Doughnut Stop and Petersville. Like that kid, what was his name?"

"Gus," Zoe said.

"Right, Gus. It would be so perfect."

"No. Way."

"Do you realize how selfish you're being? You won't even do this for the town?"

"No."

Jeanine leaned forward into the front seat. "Do you hear this? Aren't you going to do something?"

"Like what?" Mom said.

"Like make him send an audition tape to *Can You Cut It?*"

Mom laughed. "We're not going to force one of our children to audition for a televised cooking competition."

"Talk about bad parenting. I mean—"

"Jeanine! *Sa soo fee!*" Dad barked.

None of us speak French, but you can't live with my father and not figure out that those words mean "cut it out." Dad only

French-es when he's angry, so it's not as if we need, or even want, an exact translation.

Jeanine sat back and gave the back of Dad's head a dirty look.

That's when I asked the question I'd been waiting to ask since Jim told us about the post office: "Mom, how come The Station House stopped serving lunch?"

She didn't answer. Her elbow was leaning on the armrest and her chin was in her hand, a finger over her nose, bouncing like it was tapping out a secret code.

"Mom?"

Her finger froze mid-tap. "I told you."

"You told me it was too much work, but the work would have been worth it if people had been coming, right? I mean, wasn't part of the problem that there was no lunch business?"

Tap-tap. Tap. "The Station House is fine."

"The Station House is *great*," Dad said as if Mom had just said something he needed to set straight.

"*Mmm-hmm*. Great," Mom said, hitting the *t* all weird.

"You didn't really answer my question," I said.

"Sure we did," Dad said. And there was something about the way he said it that sounded like, "The end." "Hey, you know what I was thinking Petersville needs?"

"People?" I said.

"A newspaper. What does everyone think about *The Petersville Gazette*?" Dad's sycamore-syrup smile was taking up the whole rearview mirror.

"How is a newspaper going to help bring people to Petersville?" I asked.

"It won't, but it will improve the Petersville experience. You know, like, it will list events, provide a store guide, a map—"

"A map? Petersville has one street." My dad had worked in a bank before we moved to Petersville; couldn't he come up with an idea that might make the town some money?

"It wouldn't be to keep people from getting lost. It would be kind of like an activity guide. You know, like a 'Time Out Petersville.'"

"*Ooh*, maybe I could write for it," Jeanine said, all excited again. "Or even have a column. Could I, Dad?"

"Sure."

"It's perfect for my Young Leaders Scholarship application. 'Writes weekly newspaper column keeping town residents informed.' Talk about making an impact in your community, right?"

"Hey, Tris, you want to write an article for the newspaper?" Dad eyed me in the rearview mirror.

"No, thanks."

A writing assignment was the last thing I needed.

When we got home, everyone went upstairs except for me.

I went to the kitchen, took one of the big index cards Mom keeps for recipes, and wrote across the top, "Ideas for Making Doughnuts Faster."

Then I underlined it.

And boxed it.

And waited for the ideas to come.

They didn't.

I couldn't focus on doughnuts. All I could think about was what Jim had said, about Petersville melting away like those icebergs in the Arctic. And not just Petersville. He'd said the same thing was happening all over upstate. How had I missed that? I mean, I didn't live in the Arctic. I couldn't see the icebergs getting smaller every day, but how had I missed what was happening right in front of me?

We'd only been in Petersville since November, not even a year, but Jim said post offices and schools were closing all over upstate. What about libraries? What would Josh and his mom do if the library closed?

Were other people talking about this stuff? In other small towns like ours, at other meetings, were they doing just what we were, working out plans for survival?

And that's when it came to me, what we should be looking for: fixes that had worked. Towns that had already put survival plans into action.

Ice cream. I needed ice cream. I think better with ice cream. I'm pretty sure everyone does. I don't know the science behind it, but computers have those little fans to keep them from overheating, so maybe ice cream cools the brain the same way. Then again, it could just be the sugar.

I scooped myself an enormous bowl of homemade chocolate peanut butter brittle—Mom lets us make up our own flavors—and went upstairs to my parents' office.

The room was dark except for the glow from the computer screen. I closed the door but didn't turn on the light, then sat in the roll-y chair, and swiveled to face the computer.

HOW DO YOU STOP UPSTATE NEW YORK TOWNS FROM DISAPPEARING I typed into the Google search box.

Just so you know, I'm not a complete nuddy. It's not as if I expected Google to spit out exactly what I needed like a genie. But I'd found the more specific I could make my searches to start, the less time it took to find something useful. Part of the problem with getting results that are totally random is that sometimes before I know it, I've spent thirty minutes watching YouTube videos of people exploding doughnuts with firecrackers (there are way more of these than you would guess).

"Crumbling Ruins and Ghost Towns of Upstate New York, A Story in Pictures," was the first hit.

Clearly, not an answer, but something made me click on the slideshow anyway.

A stone bridge missing its middle flashed onto the screen, then melted into a crumpled barn with vines crawling through its windows, then melted into an indoor swimming pool overflowing with school desks—

Click.

There were more ruins to see, but I was done. Looking at places that weren't places anymore felt like sightseeing in a graveyard.

I scanned the rest of the search results:

"Where Have All the Small Towns Gone?" *Rural Intelligencer. Click.*

"The Decline of Upstate New York," *The New York Times. Click.*

"Bad News for Rural America," *Forbes. Click.*

If I wanted to understand the problem, I had everything I needed right here. Page after page, article after article, all said the same thing about the towns of upstate New York: no jobs, no people, no future.

Many scary D-words were used. Down-in-the-dumps. Dwindling. Declining. Depressed. And my favorite: Dying. Exactly what you want to hear about your hometown.

What were my parents thinking when they decided to move

to upstate New York? Had they done any research at all? They'd gotten us here just in time to see it disappear forever.

Then, on the third page, there was a hit with no D-words.

"How Tea Saved Krakow, NY," *The New York Times*.

I clicked on the link, then took a big scoop of ice cream and let it melt on the spoon in my mouth as I read.

You can't get more small-town than Krakow, New York. With just one traffic light, a gas station, and a general store, it's easy to miss as you drive through.

I bit down on the spoon. Krakow was Petersville.

The only big employer in the area for decades was the Willow Paper Co. It was Willow that kept Krakow afloat while so many other upstate New York towns were drowning.

D. Drowning.

While small compared to most, the Willow mill had plenty of jobs to keep the tiny population of Krakow employed.

Then in 2005, Willow went bankrupt. The mill closed its doors, putting 225 people out of work. Krakow was in serious trouble.

Enter our hero: Alhaadi Okello, known around Krakow as "the Tea King." Okello arrived in the United States from Kenya fifteen years ago on a lottery visa with two hundred dollars in his pocket and dreams of starting a tea business. He even knew what he'd call it: Majani (the word for "leaves" in Swahili). His suitcases were packed with tea leaves from his family's farm in the Embu district of Kenya.

Today, Majani is on shelves in stores across the United States, and the company employs 203 people. Care to guess where Majani set up shop? That's right: the old Willow Paper mill.

Krakow is now thriving. For the first time in years, the town is growing. Stop anybody on Main Street and ask what saved Krakow, you'll get the same answer: the Tea King.

I must have forgotten about the spoon in my mouth because the next thing I knew, it clattered to the floor. I froze, listening for sounds in the hall, but all I heard was the wind chasing itself around the house. I let out the breath I'd been holding and went back to the article.

I had to start from the beginning again, mostly because I couldn't believe it. This man came to upstate New York from Africa and started a big-time tea company in a dying town in the middle of nowhere?

Yes, somehow, he had.

"I didn't know about this area," Okello confesses as he pumps gas into his car on Krakow's Main Street. "A friend saw this advertisement for the mill building and we drove up here from New Jersey to see. Nobody else wanted this place. It was a very good deal. I think the bank thought so too, and that's why they helped me buy it." He smiles and waves to a family in a truck that has just pulled up.

Tea experts say that while there are plenty of tea companies that use leaves from Kenya, Majani is one of the finest. "It's made a big name for itself selling purple tea," says Abby Kyle, author of It's All in the Leaves: A Tea Atlas. *"You can only get it from Kenya, and until recently, nobody was selling it in the U.S. It's got a wonderful flavor and amazing health benefits."*

Ask Okello his secret to success, he'll tell you this: "Every day in business, we hit new problems. But if we keep our minds open, we always find a solution. Maybe it isn't pretty or fancy. Maybe it's not perfect, but it works. That's what matters. Just find a way to make it work."

Majani's biggest problem now? Getting tea to everyone who wants it. "We've had a hard time keeping up with demand. But it's a good problem to have, no? We must be doing something right."

My knees were bouncing up and down.

Alhaadi Okello had saved a town with tea. Tea! Which is fine, but it's basically just leaf-flavored water. There's only so good tea can get, even if it is purple. If he could save Krakow with tea, why couldn't I save Petersville with doughnuts?

And not only was Krakow like Petersville—Majani and The Doughnut Stop were both struggling with demand.

I scrolled down.

There was a photograph of Okello: a tall man with dark brown skin and a big smile wearing an apron and a shower cap and lifting the crank on a gleaming steel tank. The caption read, *Okello demonstrates his new tea blending machine.*

That's when something clicked, and where there had been a big black hole, there was finally an idea.

I moved the cursor back up to the search box, typed in the words *DOUGHNUT MACHINE*, and held my breath.

And then it was right there in front of me, almost as if I had wished it to life: a doughnut robot.

The Belshaw Adamatic Donut Robot was the very first result. *Click.*

I had never seen anything so beautiful. It was all stainless steel and shiny. It mixed. It fried. It glazed and injected. The Donut Robot did it all.

It made ninety-six dozen doughnuts an hour.

It was perfect. It was what I needed. It was what the town needed.

I took my phone out of my pocket, snapped a photo of the computer screen, and texted it to Josh.

Me: Say hello to the answer to our problems
Josh: What is it
Me: A Donut Robot
Josh: haha
Me: No joke 96 dozen donuts per hr

Josh: We could build a donut empire
Me: That's what I was thinking
Josh: $?

I had no idea. I'd been so excited I hadn't even looked for a price.

Me: Checking

I clicked on "more information."

Me: Small problem…

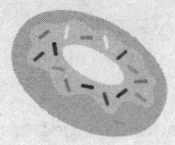
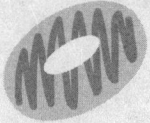

8

The Petersville Gazette

Vol. 1, Issue 1

Vol. 1, Issue 1

Town Happenings

"Main Street Makeover" needs volunteers! Petersville wants you! Come to the library to sign up. No skills necessary.

Congratulations to the winners of the "Put a Shop on Main Street" competition! Everyone is looking forward to the opening of Petersville's newest businesses:

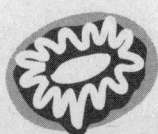

Calvin's Pop Shop! Four flavors of popcorn, air-popped fresh daily, made from Petersville's own Crooked Tree Farm corn kernels.

Stinky Cheese Farm Store! Get Riley Carter's deliciously stinky cheese right on Main Street.

The Board Room! How long has it been since you played Battleship, Candy Land, or Risk? Come to The Board Room when it opens to play these games and many others, thanks to Hazel Abernathy, who has been collecting board games since she was seven years old. Games also available for purchase.

The Watch, Cut, and Quilt! Watch your favorite movies on a big screen while you quilt or have your hair cut or both! (Haircuts by Deena Manes. Quilting by Peggi Jennings.)

An egg with four yolks—that's right, four!—was produced by one of Ron Jennings' chickens! Ron knew that egg had at least a double yolk from its size, so he asked his wife Peggi to video when he cracked it open. When four yolks spilled out, instead of scrambling them up, he decided to offer others a chance to see the wonder for themselves. The egg and all its yolks are available for viewing at the library this week and this week only. Just ask Mary at the circulation desk, as it must be stored in the refrigerator. The video will be posted on the town website (coming soon).

Featured Series

Things Most People Get Wrong and How YOU Can Get Them Right

By Jeanine Levin

Anybody ever heard you can't have dessert when it's late because it will make you hyper? Guess what? Scientists have studied the effects of sugar on kids and have found it does not impact behavior.

Parents, sugar does NOT make kids hyper, so stop saying that it does.

Kids, don't let your parents skimp on dessert after dinner. Knowledge is power.

You're welcome!

The Donut Robot was the perfect fix. It did everything we could possibly need it to do and more. We'd be able to make enough doughnuts to sell them all over upstate New York if we wanted to. There was just one problem. It cost $50,000.

How were two twelve-year-olds going to get that kind of money?

We found the answer in *Starting Your Own Business for Dummies*, page 124: "Need money to expand your business? Time to pitch to investors."

We'd pitched to investors before, to get money to start The Doughnut Stop, but that had been way simpler. For one thing, we didn't need anything close to $50,000. For another, we were pitching to my parents. I couldn't ask my parents for that kind of money even if I thought they had it, which I was pretty sure they didn't.

Josh and I wrote pitch emails to every big company on the planet we thought might be interested in a doughnut business. I even wrote one to that guy who started Amazon. I knew it was a long shot, but I'd heard he was getting into food, and he seemed like someone who'd appreciate a good product even if it was made by a seventh grader. Josh had the idea to write to a couple of movie stars who'd grown up in upstate New York.

A month later, we were nowhere. With the exception of an actor

I'd never heard of who was interested only if we put a picture of his face on our package—as if we even had a doughnut package—nobody even replied.

We had no idea what to try next, and we were fried. We were back at school, writing all these emails, making doughnuts, and running the shop. And since the *Destination Eating* article had come out, we were selling out faster than ever. I'd stopped looking at the comments on our website.

The only good news: Jim's "Main Street Makeover" was really moving along. It wasn't as if I thought people were going to vacation in Petersville just so they could get a haircut, watch a movie, and make a quilt all at once. But the Watch, Cut, and Quilt was way better than an empty shop, and definitely more unusual than a place where you could do just one of those things. Besides, people took road trips to see weird things all the time, right? Like to visit the world's largest fish statue or that Eiffel Tower made of spaghetti. Maybe Petersville could become like one of those places.

The stores weren't up and running yet. Volunteers were still cleaning out the buildings. It wasn't just a question of sweeping and mopping. They were packed full of seriously old stuff, like many, many unopened boxes of something called "The Baby Alice Thumb Guard," a device to keep kids from sucking their thumbs. From the picture, I'm pretty sure you'd be arrested today for putting one of those on your kids, so it's not as if we could sell them on eBay or anything. Some stuff could be used, but most of it had to be hauled to the dump.

On a crazy hot Friday in May, after we'd sold out of doughnuts, Dr. C roped me and Josh into painting. Every building on Main Street was getting a new coat of paint, and judging from the colors Dr. C had chosen, he was definitely working the don't-miss-a-visit-to-the-wackiest-small-town-on-earth angle. Each side of every building on Main Street would be painted a different color.

"But they'll all have the same yellow trim," Dr. C said, as we carried cans of paint from the trunk of his car to the porch of the building we were supposed to be painting.

Josh put the cans down and wiped his forehead with his T-shirt. "How come? I mean, why not just have them be totally different?"

"I like the symbolism," Dr. C said.

Josh looked at me.

I shrugged. "What does the yellow symbolize?"

"It's not about the color," Dr C said like this was completely obvious. "It's about the connection."

"Oh," Josh said. "I get it."

"You do?" I said.

"Not really," he whispered.

"Come on, guys. Think! It's not that deep. You, me." He thumped his paint-splattered, Hawaiian-shirted chest. "We're different, right?"

"Yeah," I said.

"But we're still connected, right?"

"Yeah?" I still didn't get it.

He threw his hands in the air. "Community! It symbolizes community!" Then he walked off to get more paint.

"Oh, I guess I see now," Josh said.

I did too, but I was pretty sure nobody else would unless Dr. C explained it to them as well. Maybe he could write an article about it for the paper.

As Josh and I painted the side of the building a blue-green color Dr. C called "teal," Josh told me all the new stuff he'd learned about the Tea King. He'd become a walking, talking Alhaadi Okello Wikipedia page.

"Listen to this quote I found." He put down his brush and took out his phone. "'I love to compete. I hate my competitors. You really have to love to compete to be successful in business.'"

For my sake, I hoped that wasn't true. "He sounds like Jeanine. Just remove 'business' and insert 'Geo Bee.'"

"Think about it. This guy came here with only two hundred

dollars and a suitcase full of tea leaves, and look at what he's done. And this... I don't know, I feel like he's saying, to succeed, he had to be tough, to want to fight, you know, like he was prepared to do whatever it took."

"He's like a business action hero. I can see the movie trailer now."

Josh laughed. "But he is, kind of, you know? I mean, he's a total hero to the people who live in that town."

I'd been joking, but I was with Josh. Even though nobody would ever make a movie about Alhaadi Okello, the Tea King was a hero.

"Hey, did you read that stuff I sent you?"

"I read some of it." I'd still be reading if I'd read everything Josh had found on Okello.

"Did you read that interview he did with the *Albany Times*?"

"I don't think so."

"You need to read that one. Okay?"

"Okay," I promised.

At dinner that night, I could barely keep my eyes open. Between getting up at 5:30 that morning to make doughnuts before school, a full day of classes, working at The Doughnut Stop, and then painting in the heat, I couldn't wait to crawl into bed. The problem was when I got up from the table, I didn't have the energy to drag myself up there.

My room isn't just upstairs, it's in the attic, and I couldn't face the stairs and the rope ladder that lay between me and my bed. I'd need a pit stop.

I went into the living room and flopped onto the couch.

The laptop was sitting open on the coffee table, and I pulled it onto my chest.

Typing lying down like that was slow, but eventually, I found the article Josh had wanted me to read. In the interview, the Tea King was talking about how Majani was Krakow, and that it was the people there who had made the company such a success: *Start a business in a place like Krakow, a struggling town in upstate New York, and you don't just get employees—you get partners who work around the clock with you, who make your dream their own, and will not rest until they make it come true. This is the reason to start a business in these towns or to give money to someone who wants to. All they need is a good idea…*

I was suddenly wide awake.

I clicked open Google and put four words in the search box: *Alhaadi Okello contact information.*

You probably aren't surprised that I couldn't find the Tea King's direct email address, but I did find one for someone in the Majani Press Office, Wally Siglinder.

To: WSiglinder@MajaniTea.com
From: DoughnutBoy@TheDoughnutStop.com
Subject: Urgent Investment Opportunity

Dear Mr. Siglinder,
    It would be great if you could forward this email to Mr. Okello.

Dear Mr. Okello,
    I really hope this email gets to you and that you actually read it. I don't mean that in a rude way at all, like you think you're too good to read random emails from 12-year-old kids. I just know that you're busy trying to get Majani into every store in America.
    I don't want to freak you out, but we actually have a lot in common:
    1. We both come from food families (you=tea business, me=restaurant business)

2. We both came to upstate NY from other places (you=Kenya, me=NYC)

3. We both own businesses in upstate NY (you= Majani, me=The Doughnut Stop).

4. We both want to use our businesses to keep upstate NY towns from going extinct.

So Majani is a lot further along than The Doughnut Stop in meeting its goals. I'm not making excuses, but you should know that me and my cofounder are in seventh grade, which makes some things difficult.

Right now, our biggest problem is keeping up with demand. I read that Majani has also struggled with this. The only way to really increase our supply is to buy the Belshaw Donut Robot, which can make over 1,000 doughnuts in an hour. The problem is it costs $50,000.

I know you're focused on expanding Majani, so I completely understand if you can't help us out, but I read something you said that made me think maybe you'd be interested in investing in The Doughnut Stop. It was about funding businesses in places like Krakow. Maybe you don't remember because it seems like you give a lot of interviews, and my friend Josh has read all of them. Anyway, I was wondering whether you would fund us, The Doughnut Stop, because Petersville, my town, really needs this business and may not be a town for much longer unless we can change things.

Don't think I'm asking for a handout. I've read *Starting Your Own Business for Dummies*, and I know how these things work. We got investors when we opened The Doughnut Stop, and we paid them all back and they even made some money.

I know this is a lot to ask, but I just thought if you really believed what you said, you might want a chance to help us out. We have a great product. I'm attaching an article *Destination Eating* did on us, and our latest profit-and-loss report. We may be in the seventh grade, but we run The Doughnut Stop like a real business.

I hope I'll hear from you but, don't worry, it's not as if I'm expecting anything to come from this email. Do you ever just feel like you have to try something even when it seems impossible?

Thanks for reading this.

Sincerely,
Tris Levin
Co-Owner of The Doughnut Stop
Petersville, NY

I read it through once more, then hit Send.

I was just about to close the laptop when I noticed I had a new email. It was from an address I didn't recognize. The subject line read: Congratulations!

Finally, some good news. I clicked it open.

To: DoughnutBoy@TheDoughnutStop.com,
   NerdyandProud@mar.com
From: CTeam@CYCl.com
Subject: Congratulations!

Tristan,

Congratulations! The *Can You Cut It?* team loved your audition video, and we'd like you to come in for a callback on May 14 at 10:00 a.m.

In the attachment, you'll find detailed information about the callback, filming schedule (should you be selected), and consent forms for parental signature.

Please reply to this email as soon as possible to confirm that you will be attending the callback.

We look forward to meeting you!

All the best,
Randy Merriman
Producer
Can You Cut It?™

Was this a joke?

I opened the attachment. It was ten pages in tiny print with very long words. Definitely not a joke.

I read the email again.

That's when I saw it, the other email address in the To box: NerdyandProud@mar.com.

"Jeanine!"

"What?" She came out of the kitchen sucking a Popsicle.

"You sent an audition tape to *Can You Cut It?*"

"Did we get a callback?" She crossed her fingers.

"Uh, yeah?" I was in shock. This was too much even for Jeanine.

"Yes!" She spun around spraying the room with Popsicle juice. "Tris has a callback for *Can You Cut It?!*" she yelled into the kitchen.

A second later, Mom and Dad were reading the email over my shoulder.

"This is so exciting!" Mom said super loud right in my ear.

"It's not exciting because I'm not doing it."

"I'll do it," Zoe said. She was sitting on the carpet with Henry in her lap trying to force-feed him a Popsicle.

"I don't understand. Why don't you want to do it now?" Dad said.

"Now? I never wanted to do it. Ms. NerdyandProud made the video and sent it in without asking me."

"You should see it," Jeanine said. "Kevin taught me how to use iMovie, and I edited together all these clips of Tris cooking, even from when he was really little. You know the one where he's like three and naked with the apron and—"

"You didn't!" This was not happening.

"Oh, I love that video. You were so cute," Mom said, cupping my chin in her palm.

I swiped her hand away. "Mom! Focus! Jeanine went behind my back when she *knew* I didn't want this. It's just…wrong and… messed up!" I was so angry I could barely speak.

"The only reason you didn't want to try is because you were afraid they wouldn't want you, but they do," Jeanine said between licks of Popsicle.

"Look, we get it," Dad said. "She shouldn't have done this without your permission."

"You think?" I said.

"But—" Dad added.

"But what?"

"But regardless of how it happened, it's a great opportunity as long as you don't take it too seriously."

"And you're so perfect for it!" Mom said, still way too loud.

"*And....*" Jeanine raised her Popsicle to make her point. "It's great publicity for Petersville and The Doughnut St—"

"No!" I stood up. "Why aren't any of you listening? It's my choice, and I'm not doing it."

Then I got out of there before they could say anything else.

I had just flopped onto my bed when Jeanine climbed out of the hole in the floor where the ladder leads up to my room.

"Go. Away." I put a pillow over my head.

"Have you even thought about the prize money? You could use it for your doughnut machine."

I threw the pillow at her. "Doughnut robot, not doughnut machine."

"Whatever. If you win, you could buy it."

"The chances I'd win—"

"But you *could*. You know you're as good as those kids, better even."

I definitely never would have messed up the finger test like Jackson, but cooking skills weren't my problem.

I sat up. "Look, I just can't do it."

Jeanine dropped onto the bed next to me. "Is this like prime buzz?"

I pulled my knees up to my chest. "No."

It totally was.

"You know, nobody believed you were sick all those times."

"What's prime buzz?" Zoe asked, her head popping up through the hole in the floor.

"It's a math game you play in school," Jeanine said. "You go around the room counting. The first person is one, then the next is two, like that, but if your number is prime, you say, 'buzz,' instead of the number."

Zoe ran across the room and jumped onto the bed. "What's prime?"

"A number divisible only by itself and one," Jeanine said.

"What's 'divisible'?"

Jeanine rolled her eyes. "I'll show you tomorrow. The point is, Tris doesn't like to play."

"No, the point is, nobody likes to play except Jeanine," I said.

"Whatever, nobody but *Tris* pretends to get sick just so they don't have to play."

"I *wasn't* pretending."

Playing that stupid game actually made me sick. There was something about having to figure something out with everyone watching that made my brain feel like it was churning through chewing gum. And Jeanine was right. *Can You Cut It?* was exactly the same. No matter how much prep you did, you'd have to come up with recipes on the spot in front of everybody, and when you failed, you'd do it in front of Chef JJ, the other kids, and millions of TV viewers. "Why don't *you* do it? It's just like your Solve-a-Thons and Geography Bees, and you rock those."

"Cooking's your thing, not mine," Jeanine said.

"Yeah, Jeanine would never cut it," Zoe said.

Jeanine scooted around so she was facing me. "Look, so you don't like to compete. Get over it. Do you really want to give up this chance to go on television and tell millions of people to come visit Petersville, *plus* the chance to buy your doughnut robot? You want to throw all that away without even trying?"

No, I didn't.

What I wanted was to be the Doughnut King of Petersville. And now there was a way. Was I really too scared to give it a shot?

I wrote the Tea King we had all this stuff in common, but he did whatever it took. Was I going to give up without a fight? I'd never become the Doughnut King like that. I'd be plain old Tris forever.

"Fine, I'll do it."

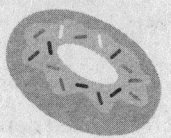
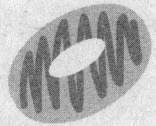

9

The callback guidelines said I had to bring a dish of my own creation. I could make anything so, big surprise, I was making doughnuts—butterscotch cream-filled ones because I thought they'd score highest in the categories that counted:

1. Creativity: I'd made up the recipe for butterscotch cream myself, and the doughnut had my secret ingredient: mashed potatoes. Also, I'd never seen butterscotch doughnuts anywhere else, and Chef JJ gives extra points for originality.
2. Yumminess: They always sold out first. Clearly, yummy.
3. Presentation: This was the one weakness. I planned to roll it in a sugar-vanilla mixture, but there really wasn't much *wow*. It was all just kind of tan. Pretty *blah*, but there's only so much

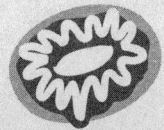

you can do to change the look of a cream-filled doughnut, and using food coloring is considered a cheap trick.

Besides telling us we had to bring something we'd made, the show didn't give us much information about the callback. I didn't even know how many kids got callbacks. They did tell us a bit about the season format though. It would cover four different regional competitions—I was competing to be in the East Coast one—and the winners of each of those would go on to compete against each other in the finale for the prize money.

On the day of the callback, I got up early, put on my PETERSVILLE, THE PLACE TO EAT T-shirt, and went downstairs to make the doughnuts fresh before we drove to the city.

Making the doughnuts gave me something to focus on, but as soon as I finished and sat down for breakfast, I started to get that "prime buzz" feeling.

My insides were spinning, so I just sat there staring at my charred French toast. Mom had been weirdly off her game since the town meeting.

Dad could smile all he wanted. Mom was not fine.

"Eat!" Jeanine tapped my plate with her knife.

"I'm not hungry."

"Nervous?" Mom asked.

I shrugged.

Jeanine tapped the plate again. "Not eating is a rookie mistake. Eating a good breakfast before competition is key. Solve-a-Thon. Spelling Bee. Cooking reality show. It's all the same. You need to feed the brain."

I cut a piece of toast and ate it. All I tasted was ash. No amount of maple syrup would cover it up, but sweet, sticky ash had to be better than flaky, dry ash. I reached for the bottle and poured.

"Oh, and don't forget to visualize success," Jeanine added. "That's key. You have to picture yourself attaining your goal. Believe and achieve."

"Did you get that from Yoda? 'Do. Or do not. There is no try,'" I said in my best Yoda voice.

Jeanine rolled her eyes. "Think about it. How can you do something if don't *believe* you can do it?"

I looked at my plate and tried to see Chef JJ handing me my *Can You Cut It?* apron in the pool of syrup.

"Don't just look at it. Eat it! We gotta go." Jeanine was coming to the city because she'd arranged for her friend, Kevin, to meet us for dinner after the callback.

Zoe had wanted to come too, but the last time we'd driven to Manhattan, she'd filled three vomit buckets, and nobody wanted to relive that, not even for dinner at China Palace.

Dad seemed perfectly happy to stay home with his face glued to his laptop. People had really flipped for his newspaper, especially people whose names showed up in it. I thought the newspaper was okay, but I didn't see why he couldn't do something else too, something more useful for the town. I didn't care how amazing a newspaper might be, it couldn't keep a place from disappearing. Besides, how much time could he spend reporting news in Petersville anyway? It wasn't as if chickens lay eggs with four yolks every day.

By 8:15 a.m., we were already crossing the bridge from the Bronx into Manhattan. Jeanine hadn't stopped talking the whole way. She had some idea about making Petersville into a colonial living history museum with costumes and theme food and games.

"I don't care, Jeanine. I'm not putting mutton on the menu," Mom shouted over the air whooshing through the station wagon. The air-conditioning was broken, so we'd rolled down all the windows, which meant we'd been yelling at each other for the last two hours.

"But mutton was what they would have served in 1627," Jeanine shot back.

"Jeanine, I told you," my mother shouted at the rearview mirror,

"The Station House could do some Colonial-themed dishes, but we're not serving mutton."

"And I'm not changing The Doughnut Stop to The Olycakes Stop." According to Jeanine, that's what the Dutch colonists called doughnuts. "Hey, Mom, isn't mutton just lamb?" I was hoping if I could get Mom to do what Jeanine wanted, she'd stop hassling me.

"It's *old* lamb," Mom said. "Old and chewy and has a flavor that kind of screams, 'flesh.'"

"Yum." We came around a bend and stopped in a line of cars that stretched as far down the West Side Highway as I could see. "Do you think maybe we should take the streets?"

"We're getting off soon anyway." She leaned out the open window, turned her face to the sun, and closed her eyes. "I can't believe you're going to meet JJ. I was trying to remember how long it's been since I've seen her. It's got to—"

"Maybe you could *call* it mutton but *use* lamb," Jeanine yelled from the back seat.

Mom opened her eyes. "Jeanine, I said no."

Just then, my pocket buzzed. I pulled out my phone.

Josh: I've been thinking. Once we have the Donut Robot,
we'll need to hire drivers to get the donuts to stores

Me: I'm not even on the show yet!!!!!

Josh: U r going to get on and u r going to win

"Don't count on it," I typed, then suddenly remembered what Jeanine had said about how it was impossible to do something you didn't believe you could do and I got worried I was jinxing myself, so I deleted it.

Me: 😊 🎉

In the rearview mirror, I could see Jeanine flipping through *A Cultural History of Pre-Revolutionary America*. "What about… pease porridge?"

"Mmm. That sounds even tastier than chewy flesh," I said. "What could be better that pea oatmeal?"

"It's not cereal. It's a savory—that means not sweet."

"I know what savory means."

"'Pease porridge is a savory pudding dish made of boiled legumes,'" Jeanine read. "'Usually split yellow or Carlin peas, with water, salt, and spices, and often cooked with a bacon or ham joint.'"

"I'm not making pease porridge either." Mom honked at a car trying to cut in front of us.

Jeanine turned the page. "What about boiled meat?"

"Another winner," I said.

Jeanine knocked me on the head with the book. "Whose side are you on?"

"*Ow!* The side without boiled meat."

Mom put the car in Park and turned around. "No boiled meat, no pease porridge, no mutton. *I* will come up with some themed dishes if and when I have the time, and if Jim gives this whole idea a green light."

Jeanine slammed the book shut. "What about changing the name? Like instead of The Station House, you could call it The Station House Tavern."

Mom turned around and put the car back into Drive.

"Mom?"

Mom leaned her head back on her seat and closed her eyes again. "I think JJ will recognize me. I mean, I don't look *that* different."

"Mom!" Jeanine shouted.

"Oh, fine!" Mom scowled at the rearview mirror. "I'll think about changing the name to The Station House Tavern."

"Thank you." Jeanine grinned and went back to reading her book. Mom closed her eyes again.

I opened the box on my lap to check the doughnuts, as if somehow they were going to escape when I wasn't looking.

Yup, still there.

A short time later, we turned off the highway. Buildings, people, and cars flew by in a noisy, squirming swirl.

That first moment back in New York always feels like the city's dials have been cranked up while I've been away. Everything's too loud, too bright, too colorful.

When we hit Fifth Avenue, Mom headed downtown. "It's Fifty-First, right?"

"Yeah." I gripped my box a little tighter.

"Six-One-One. There it is." Jeanine pointed to a building with a gleaming brass entrance and a big fountain out front.

I could already feel my heart thudding at the back of my throat, and we hadn't even gone inside.

"Paperwork?" The woman behind the desk put out a hand. A huge blowup of Chef JJ's face next to CAN YOU CUT IT? in shiny red letters covered the wall behind her.

"I keep this." She put my paperwork on a pile. "And you take this." She slipped a card with my name on it into a plastic holder on a string and handed it to me.

I held it up to Jeanine. "Tristan? Really? The least you could have done was put Tris."

"What? It's your name."

"You have to put it on," the woman said.

"Oh, right. Sorry." I looped the string over my head. It reminded me of those tags they made us wear when we went on field trips in preschool (*If found, please return this child to West Side Playgroup*).

"Tristan?" A woman in a flowing gray dress was holding open a glass door opposite the receptionist's desk "Would you follow me please? Your family can come too." She smiled like she was on a toothpaste commercial.

As we followed her through a maze of hallways, Samara explained how the callbacks worked. "So I'm just leading you to a lounge where you can relax with the other kids and their families. Then we'll bring you out two at a time for your interview with Marco—he's one of the producers—and your meeting with Chef JJ. That's where you'll present your food." She stopped at a glass-walled seating area.

"When does he find out if he made it?" Jeanine asked.

"Actually, this is our last set of callbacks for the East Coast competition, and we're on a tight schedule, so we'll decide this afternoon. You'll hear by tomorrow at the latest."

"Thanks." At least the news, good or bad, would come quick.

I didn't want to be too obvious checking out the competition, but from a quick scan of the room, I guessed there were about ten contestants. Since we all had family with us, it was pretty packed.

We circled a few times, trying to find three seats together. In the end, we let Mom take an armchair by the TV, which was playing the show's greatest hits on a loop, and Jeanine and I squeezed onto a couch on the other side of the room.

"Hey, watch it!" somebody said as I scooted back on the sofa.

I turned and found myself face-to-face with a steaming Starbucks cup. The girl holding it had freckled brown skin, dangly earrings shaped like whisks, and a seriously annoyed look on her face.

"Sorry. Do you need a napkin or something?"

"Not unless you're going to make another run at spilling it." She blew into the cup and sipped. As she drank, my eyes drifted to the buttons covering her jean jacket: *Come to the dark side—we have cookies*; *"BBQ may not be the road to world peace, but it's a start."—Anthony Bourdain…*

"Whatcha got?" she asked.

"Huh?"

She pointed to the box.

"Oh, doughnuts."

"You mean like at Dunkin' Donuts."

"No. Not like Dunkin' Donuts." This girl would laugh in my face if I told her these were life-changing doughnuts. "These are… different, and they're filled with butterscotch cream."

"*Ooo*, butterscotch cream," she said in a voice that made clear she still wasn't impressed. "Can I see?"

I opened the box.

"Not very pretty, are they?"

"Okay, that's it!" Jeanine stood up. "Move!"

"What?" I said.

"Up! Now!"

Before I knew it, Jeanine had pulled me off the couch and was dragging me to the other side of the room.

"What's your problem?"

"Don't you know what trash talk is?" Jeanine said, searching the room for open seats.

"Did you hear what that girl said?"

"Uh, yeah, I heard what she said. She was trash-talking you. Classic trash talk. Newsflash: she wants you to think you don't have a chance. She wants you to give up before you even start. Look at these kids—that's what they all want. *Duh*. You're the competition. Solve-a-Thon, cooking competition, it's all the same. Never, ever listen to the competition about anything."

We found a small sliver of space on a couch by the door. "I can sit on the armrest," I said.

"Oh, no need for that, hon, we can scooch," said a woman with bright yellow hair and sparkly lips. "Move over, Immy." She shooed the girl next to her. "See, plenty of room. I'm Ingrid, and this is my daughter, Imogen."

Imogen had the same hair and lips as her mom, but was also wearing a pink toque.

In case your mom isn't a chef, a toque is one of those tall hats that chefs wear. Because my mom *is* a chef, I can also tell you that there are one hundred folds in a toque for the hundred ways you can cook an egg. Just a fun fact.

"Thanks." I sat. "I'm Tris. And this is my sister, Jeanine."

Jeanine squeezed in next to me. "Imogen, are you aware of the bias against female chefs in professional kitchens? Do you really think girly toques help?"

"Jeanine, they were being nice," I whispered. "They weren't trash-talkers."

Jeanine turned her back on Imogen and Ingrid. "No, they're not trash-talkers. They're krill. Do you want to be krill or do you want to be a shark?"

"Krill?"

"You know, krill, the fish that all the other fish eat. Do you want to be krill, or do you want to be a shark, the fish all the other fish fear?"

"Are those my only choices?"

"You think this is a joke? Nobody wins something like this by accident. You understand that, right?"

"It's not like I'm not prepared."

"I'm not talking cooking skills. I'm talking attitude."

"Fine. I get it." And I did. I had to channel the Tea King. *I love to compete… I love to compete…*

Every twenty minutes or so, Samara would come back to drop off two kids and take two more. After about an hour, Mom wandered over.

"I was just thinking," she said as she sat between me and Jeanine. Imogen and her mom were gone by then, so there was space. "If you *do* meet JJ today, definitely tell her who you are. I think—no, I'm sure she'll remember me, and Walter too."

"Like *that's* going to get him on the show?" Jeanine said.

"It can't hurt. I mean, who knows how many kids they called back in total. It might help to have something to make him stand out."

"Thanks, Mom. Great pep talk." Did she think my doughnuts weren't good enough to make me stand out?

"I didn't mean… Those are spectacular doughnuts, and you

know I love them. It's just we don't even know how many kids they've seen. I'm sure eventually you all just blend together in a blur, you know?"

"Can we please just drop it? You're actually making me even more nervous."

"*Ah-ha!*" Jeanine wagged a finger in my mother's face. "See, it's *not* just me. *This* is why I don't let you take me to competitions anymore."

"I don't mean to." Mom frowned. "Should I go back to where I was before?"

"No," I said. "But let's just not talk."

And we didn't for another whole half hour, not even Jeanine, which has to be some kind of record for her.

"Tristan Levin?" Samara called from the door.

"Here." I grabbed my box.

"Harper Gonzalez?"

The trash-talker from earlier stood up on the other side of the room. Just my luck.

"Have fun," Mom said. "And just, well, just remember what I told you."

"*Mom!*" Jeanine shushed my mother and pulled me in close.

"Jeanine, I got to go."

"Say it," she ordered.

"Say what?"

"You know." She looked around like she was about to divulge the secret formula for Coke, then leaned in and whispered, "Believe and achieve."

"Oh, jeez."

"Say it!" She stomped her foot.

"Inside. I'm saying it inside."

"Not good enough."

"Believe and achieve," I said into the collar of my T-shirt.

"Amazing, right? It's like magic, the way it makes you feel just saying it," she said.

"Oh, yeah. Amazing."

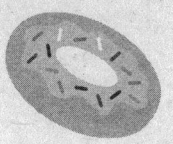

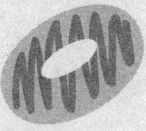

10

Samara sent Harper to meet with Chef JJ while I met with a producer named Marco, a guy with small silver hoops in his ears and a T-shirt so tight you could see his muscles bulging through it.

We chatted for a while. He wanted to know about Petersville and The Doughnut Stop. Then he asked me a bunch of questions, none of which had anything to do with food. Mostly he'd say stuff, and then I was supposed to tell him whether what he said was true for me, like this:

Marco: I like everyone I meet.
Me: No.
Marco: I want to be famous.
Me: I don't think so.

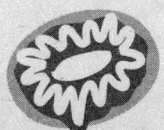

Marco: Yes or no.

Me: No. Yes—no. Sorry. It's no.

Marco: I like horror movies.

Me: Yes.

Marco: Winning isn't everything.

Me: Yes. Or I mean, it's not everything.

If I did well or badly, Marco wasn't telling. His face stayed blank the whole time. He reminded me of those guys in movies who give lie detector tests.

When I came out of the room, Harper and Samara were waiting. Then Harper went in with Marco, and Samara led me across the hall into a large room with a wall of windows.

Behind a glass table shaped like the letter C, Chef JJ sat alone looking out at the city massaging her shaved head. The sun was already melting behind the buildings, and above it, the sky was swirled like rainbow sherbet.

"This is Tristan Levin from Petersville, New York." Samara put my paperwork on the table and left.

Chef JJ flipped through my packet. And flipped some more. And made a few notes. And flipped back to the beginning.

Was this a test? Was I supposed to just start talking or present my doughnut?

I opened the box and tipped it forward so she could see inside if she looked up. "This is a—"

She put up her white, bony hand like a stop sign. "I see here your mother owns a restaurant. She isn't, by any chance, Kira Levin?"

"Oh, uh, yeah, she is." It never crossed my mind that Chef JJ would just make the connection without my saying anything.

A slow smile spread from one side of her mouth to the other. "Kira Levin. How is she?"

"She's good."

"Does she ever see Walter?"

"Actually, they run a restaurant together. In Petersville." This was good, right? We were making small talk. I could do this.

"They run it together? *Aw*."

"Uh, yeah." I really wasn't sure what to say, but it seemed like a good idea to keep the back-and-forth going.

"I haven't seen either of them for years. Did your mom tell you they both used to work for me?"

"Uh-huh."

"And you're Kira's son?"

"Uh-huh." Didn't we already cover that?

"And you want to be on *Can You Cut It?*"

"I've been cooking since I could walk, and I've watched every show. Plus, I have my own doughnut business."

Another slow smile snaked across her face. "Right, so what do we have here?"

I slid the box across the table. "This is a butterscotch cream doughnut, my original recipe for both the doughnut and the cream."

Chef JJ peered into the box and sniffed. "When did you make this?"

"This morning."

She picked up the doughnut and took a small bite, so small she didn't even hit cream.

I watched her face as she chewed. It didn't read *yuck* or *yum* or even *interesting*. Just blank like Marco's. Maybe they practiced together.

She put the doughnut back in the box and closed it.

"Oh, but you haven't tasted the—"

She put up her hand. "We're done."

That was it?

At the very least she should take another bite to get to the butterscotch. You didn't get the full effect without the cream. "Just, I don't think—"

"Please tell your mother and Walter, I said, 'hello.'" She pushed the box back across the table.

So this really was it. "Um, okay. Bye." I picked up the box, turned around, and headed for the door.

"See you soon!" she said as I stepped out into the hallway.

Wait, did that mean what I think it meant?

"This is *very* exciting!" Mom's smile was so big, her face looked like it was going to crack in half. "Isn't it exciting, Ma?"

We'd gotten the official call from *Can You Cut It?* when we got to Grandma Esme's apartment, and Mom hadn't stopped talking about it since. By the end of our ride to Chinatown, everyone on our subway car had congratulated me.

"What's the name of that tofu dish I love?" Grandma Esme asked, browsing the menu as we waited for a table at China Palace.

"I'm just so proud of you." Mom gave me a squeeze.

I forced myself to smile back at her. I must have looked like one of those clowns with the painted-on grins.

"How awesome is it that Tris is going to be on *Can You Cut It?*" Jeanine said to her friend Kevin.

"So awesome," Kevin said.

"It was my idea, you know?" she said.

"Such a great idea," Kevin said.

"Right? It's going to be fantastic publicity for Petersville," she said.

My pocket buzzed for the fifth time since I'd left the studio, and just like the other times, I didn't do anything about it. I couldn't handle more people celebrating me for something I hadn't done. Chef JJ hadn't even eaten enough of my doughnut to judge it. Did I have the guts to go on the show when I knew there was no way I'd gotten on because of my cooking skills?

"*So*, did you tell Chef JJ who you were?" Mom asked.

"Um, yeah. She says…hi."

"It's going to be so much fun to catch up with her." Mom looked happier than I'd seen her in weeks.

"Kira, the tofu dish? The crispy one?" Grandma Esme waved the menu in Mom's face.

"Salt and pepper, Ma."

"Right. Salt and pepper." Grandma Esme's eyes lit up. It's no secret where my family's food obsession comes from. "And what's the name of the duck dish I hate?"

One more family speaking rapid-fire Chinese squeezed through the narrow entrance into the crowded space between the door, the register, the lobster tank, and the golden, roast ducks hanging in the window.

"What number are we?" I figured talking about anything other than the show was a good plan.

Mom grabbed my head and kissed it. "I'm just so…happy."

Plan clearly not working.

"Believe and achieve." Jeanine nodded knowingly. "Works every time."

"Oh, yeah. Believe and achieve." Kevin gave me a double thumbs-up.

"Was it the Tea-Drunk Duck?" Grandma Esme asked, poking my mother's shoulder.

"No, it was the Gambler's Duck."

"Right. Gambler's Duck." Grandma Esme leaned over the counter. "Excuse me, do you know how much longer? We're number twenty-one."

"Sorry, lots of big parties tonight," the man said and hurried away.

"Ma, you want to go outside, get some air?"

"But we'll lose our spot."

"The kids are here. They'll come get us, right?"

"Sure," I said.

Mom handed me the slip of paper with our number on it and led Grandma Esme out of the restaurant.

Jeanine, Kevin, and I let the crowd jostle us out from its center until we were pressed against the lobster tank. The three of us turned around and watched the half-dead lobsters drifting through the purple-lit water.

"Washington," Kevin said suddenly.

"Adams," Jeanine answered.

"Jefferson."

"Madison."

"Monroe."

"What are you doing?" I said.

"Naming the presidents in order," Jeanine said.

"Yeah, I got that. Why?"

"Because it's fun. Ignore him," she said to Kevin. "Adams the Second."

"Jackson…"

Buzz. I put my hand over my pocket and let my head tip forward, knocking into the cool glass of the lobster tank. Something burned in the back of my throat like I'd eaten too much tomato sauce.

"I don't know if I can do it," I said to a lobster floating by.

"Do what?" Jeanine said.

So I told her and Kevin about my meeting with Chef JJ.

"*And?*" Jeanine said when I was done.

"*And so* I don't deserve my spot."

Jeanine crossed her arms. "Yes, you do. It doesn't matter why she chose you, just whether you're good enough to be there, which we all know you are."

"Hey." Kevin tugged Jeanine's sleeve. "Remember what my dad told us about causation? This is really a causation issue, right?"

"Oh, totally." Jeanine nodded, then turned to me. "Kevin's dad is a lawyer."

"No kidding." I rolled my eyes. How could I forget? She'd only told me a million times. "Still not following."

"The point is," Kevin said, "you're asking the wrong question. You're asking, 'Why did I get on? Was it because Chef JJ worked with my mom?'"

"Yeah, so?"

"The question you should be asking is, 'If Chef JJ *hadn't* worked with my mom, would I have gotten on anyway?' If the answer is yes, why she chose you doesn't matter because it wouldn't have changed the result."

"Exactly." Jeanine nodded. "And we all know you would have gotten on."

"*I* don't know."

"Oh, come on, Tris!" Jeanine said.

"Look, if it makes you feel any better, my cousin works in TV," Kevin said. "And she says that people get on those shows for all kinds of reasons that have nothing to do with their cooking skills. Some kids get on just because they're cute, or because they seem like they'll pick fights, and fights are the kind of things people love to watch. Your getting on because Chef JJ knows your mom is no different from all the other reasons people get on the show that have nothing to do with cooking skills."

This did not make me feel any better. But it did possibly explain Marco's weird non-cooking-related questions.

"And what about telling people what happened at the audition?" I asked.

"I think you should focus on the competition and forget everything else. It's just a distraction," Kevin said.

"That's exactly what *I* was going to say." Jeanine giggled.

Kevin's face went red. "What were we up to?"

"Huh?" I said, because I don't speak JeanineandKevin.

"Jackson," Jeanine said.

As Jeanine and Kevin went on naming presidents, I took out my phone. There were four missed calls, all from Josh, and a bunch of texts:

Josh: Did u do it?

Josh: It has to be over by now

Josh: WHAT HAPPENED

Josh: ?????

Josh: ??!!

Winnie: How'd we do, Slick?

We. That said it all.

I clicked reply and added Josh.

Me: WE MADE IT!

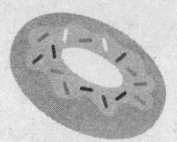

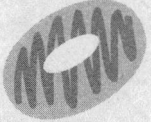

11

The Petersville Gazette

Vol. 1, Issue 5

Don't miss The Petersville Fair, Saturday, June 14! Petersville, you did it! You made over Main Street, and it looks incredible. Now it's time to celebrate. This Saturday, new stores will hold their grand openings, and special activities are planned all day:

Stinky Cheese Farm Store: Ever make your own mozzarella? It's not stinky, but it's easy and fun, and melts in your mouth.

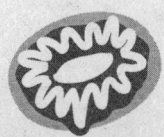

Come by the shop at 10:00 a.m. and 2:00 p.m. to give it a try.

The Watch, Cut, and Quilt: Watch *The Wizard of Oz* while Peggi shows you how to turn your old T-shirts into a cozy blanket, and Deena gives you one of her special movie-themed haircuts, "The Dorothy Trim," "The Tin Man Buzz," or "The Wizard Surprise."

The Pop Shop: Come to the fire pit in our backyard and learn how to make campfire popcorn using sticks and tinfoil.

The Board Room: Play Scrabble on a life-size board on Main Street. Board and pieces all made by Hazel herself.

The Family Clinic: Join Dr. C for free Tai Chi on the lawn outside the clinic at 8:00 a.m., 10:00 a.m., 12:00 p.m., and 2:00 p.m. Beginners welcome.

Main Street will be closed to traffic on Fair Day:

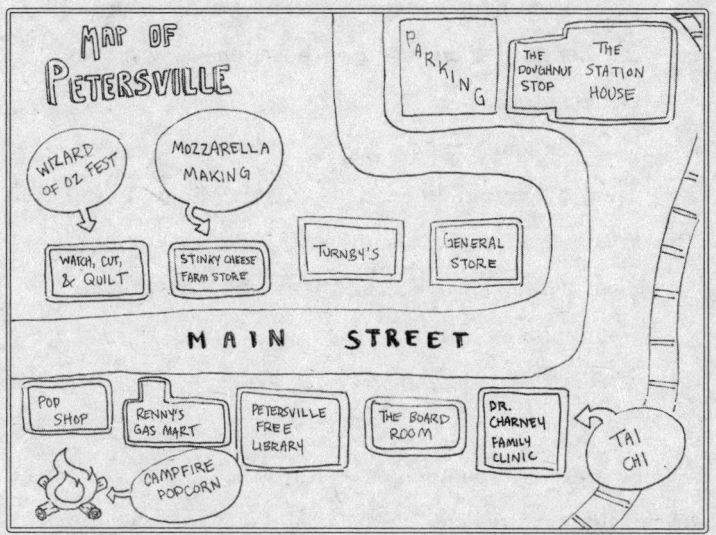

Petersville's own Tris Levin has been selected to appear on the hit TV kids' cooking competition *Can You Cut It?* The show will start filming later this month in New York City and will air in August.

Featured Series

Things Most People Get Wrong and How YOU Can Get Them Right

By Jeanine Levin

How many times have people told you to put your arms over your head when you're coughing because food or liquid has gone down the wrong pipe?

Medical experts agree that putting your arms over your head does absolutely nothing. You want to help somebody who's choking? Take a first aid class and learn how to do the Heimlich maneuver.

You're welcome!

"How late were you up?" Josh asked as he handed a customer the cinnamon pastry gun.

"No idea. Walter and I were trying to get in an extra knife skills session."

The woman on the other side of the counter held up the gun. "So I just put the tip in the hole you made and pull this trigger thing?"

Josh nodded. "Just make sure to do it slowly or you'll end up covered in cream."

She did as Josh instructed and giggled as the doughnut inflated. "This is so much fun!"

"It was his idea." Josh pointed at me.

"FYO, it's clever," she said.

"Thanks, um, I think the doughnut's had enough." Cream was dribbling out the back end.

"Oh, of course." She handed Josh the gun and took a bite. "*Mmm.*"

When she was gone, I sat on a stool behind the counter and leaned my head against the wall. "My whole life, Walter was always so chill. But ask the man to teach you what he knows about slicing and dicing, and it's like he's training you for the army. Not kidding, I think I've cut over a hundred onions."

"What's your best time?"

"Not good enough." I dropped my head on the counter. "And I don't understand—why can't I cut them into even pieces?"

"Because onions are round?"

"Still. The pieces can be *about* the same size, and I always end up with some tiny and some huge. You should see Walter's. They're perfect. And I *try* to just copy him, but the guy is like a ninja with that knife. Look at this." I held up my hands. My thumbs and the first two fingers on both hands were covered with Band-Aids.

Josh cringed.

"They look worse than they are. The real problem is that onion juice stings."

"Onion juice?"

"Yeah, you don't think of onions as juicy but the fresh ones are, and that juice kills if it gets in a cut."

Knife technique was my weakest area, but I was definitely getting better. I pretty much had the four basic cuts—the slice, the chop, the back-slice, and the rock-chop—down. The real issue now was speed. My onion chopping time was still slower than anybody who'd ever won Knife Skills Showdown, and I was less than two weeks from competition. I had to get real. There was no way I was winning that challenge. The goal now was just to get fast enough not to finish last and be eliminated.

In addition to knife skills training with Walter, I was doing two other training sessions every day: recipe creation with Mom and dish presentation with Dr. C. When I wasn't doing those or making doughnuts, I was practicing on my own, making up recipes from scratch, cooking and plating them until I was too tired to stand. I'd spent the night on the couch a few times because I was just too tired to climb up to the attic.

"I'll take a chocolate FYO," the next customer said.

"Sure." I turned to grab the gun from its hook. "Hey, who's got the cho—Zoe!"

She froze, aiming the chocolate cream pastry gun directly into her open mouth through the bars on the cage of her hockey helmet.

"But I'm hungry."

"We don't eat what we're selling while we're selling it. How many times have we said it?"

"Many?" She pulled off her helmet and hung her head.

"Maybe you just need to eat. Why don't you go ask Mom for something?"

She was almost to the door when I realized she still had the pastry gun.

"Nice try."

She made like she was putting it on a table but then broke into a run, the gun hugged to her chest. Josh cut her off, but instead of handing it over, she just hugged the gun tighter.

"Put it down," I said.

"It's almost empty. Can't I have this last little bit?"

"Zo, it's half full."

It's always seemed wrong to use tickling as a weapon, but sometimes Zoe leaves you no choice. In this case, it was just the threat of the tickle that got her to give up the gun.

After she left, a couple more customers came in, then it got quiet again. Fair Day had been way less busy than we'd all hoped.

"Are you nervous, you know, about the show?" Josh asked. "I mean, I know you're nervous, but good nervous, right? Like, excited?"

"Yeah, sure, excited nervous." Up-all-night-in-a-cold-sweat excited nervous.

There was a loud crash in the ticket office. A second later, Jeanine threw open the door.

"Why can't you just do it the way I tell you?" She was shouting and shaking her clipboard like she was about to throw it at us. "If we need something, you don't put it on the to-do list! You go into the Google Doc I created especially for orders and mark it in the appropriate square!"

"What's wrong with her?" Josh whispered.

"Jim said no to her living history museum idea. You know, the whole Colonial theme thing."

"That man has zero imagination," Jeanine snapped. "But *this* has nothing to do that! *This* is about me trying to do *my* job! And *you* making that impossible! Do you want me to quit? Do you?"

Josh looked at me. "Uh, no?" He'd spent enough time with my family to have seen plenty of Jeanine freak-outs, but they'd never been directed at him before.

"Okay then. Do you think you can manage and just! Fill! Out! The! Google! Doc!" Her face was purple.

"Sorry, Jeanine," Josh said.

"Sorry? Sorry doesn't help! Sorry never helps!"

"It's true," I whispered to Josh. "I've learned from experience, 'sorry' never makes the freak-outs less freaky."

"So what do you do when she get like this?"

"Take cover. Wait until it passes."

"Like a hurricane."

"Exactly. Hurricane Jeanine."

"You think this is funny? How funny will it be when you run out of flour!" She marched back into the ticket office and yanked the door closed with a loud crack. Then she opened it and yanked it closed again, making an even louder crack. There were two more cracks, and then silence.

"Is it over?" Josh whispered.

"Hard to say. Sometimes there are aftershocks."

"What's up Doughnut Boy?" It was Andy Hubbard, king of the Ice Kings.

"Hey, Hubb," Josh said.

"You guys have any butterscotch cream left?" He crossed his fingers.

"Yup." I took the gun down from its hook.

"How's it going in town?" Josh took out a doughnut and made a hole in the side.

"Good," Hubb said. "I mean, it's fun. It's just, you know, there aren't a ton of people."

"I don't understand why we got so few visitors." Josh shook his head. "I thought Jim ran ads in the Crellin paper and the *Albany Times*."

"He did," I said.

"My dad said he even heard Jim talk about it on 92.2," Hubb said.

"Whatever he did, it just wasn't enough," I said.

"Well, it will all change after *Can You Cut It?* Right?" Hubb knocked my shoulder with his fist.

"Oh, yeah," Josh agreed.

"I don't know," I said. "I mean, I'm going to do my best to talk up Petersville. You know, wear the T-shirt and everything, but I don't know how much of a difference it can really make. People are watching the show for the competition."

"Millions of people will hear you talk about Petersville," Hubb said. "It *has* to make a difference, right?"

Right, and that's just what was worrying me.

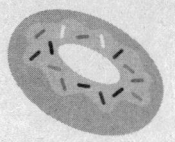
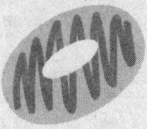

12

"Mexican. Go!" Mom spun around from the kitchen sink, clicked down the button on the stopwatch, then held up the screen with the glowing numbers so I could see them ticking by.

"Uh, chicken and…"

6…7…

"*Tick-tock,*" Zoe said through a mouthful of pasty oatmeal. It didn't matter how excited Mom was about *Can You Cut It?* She was still off her food game.

"Cut it out, Zo!"

"You know, she's actually helping," Jeanine said from the kitchen floor where she was outlining VISIT PETERSVILLE, NY! in silver paint on poster board. "It's all about getting used to real competition conditions."

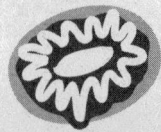

"Can everyone be quiet so I can think?"

I'd been training round the clock for the past week, ever since school broke for summer vacation. Now there were just three days left until the show, and *Can You Cut It?* was all anybody could talk about, especially since Jim had unveiled the Petersmobile, an Airstream he'd tricked out with bunk beds for nine—there were three racks held up by chains like on navy ships. He'd even gotten Dr. C to paint a mural of Petersville on its sides, complete with all the shops on Main Street and the mountains that rise above the town. An old-timey airplane flew across the sky above the mountains pulling a sign that said, *Petersville: Sometimes the Best Things Come in the Smallest Packages. Visit once and you'll want to stay forever!*

Jim had won the Airstream years ago at a county fair, and besides a few road trips down to Florida, it had sat unused in his front yard. But the idea to turn it into the Petersmobile? That was all Josh.

And it was genius, even Jeanine thought so. It was also wacky and embarrassing, but still genius, guaranteed to generate exactly the kind of buzz we needed.

Get this: we were going to sleep in it, parked right in front of The Food Connection on Fifth Avenue for the entire time I was on the show. And by "we," I mean, Jim, Winnie, Josh, and my whole family. Jim and Winnie would go back to Petersville after the first day or so though. After all, somebody had to run The Doughnut Stop.

While I was on set, the Petersmobile Team would hang out in the plaza in front of the building wearing their PETERSVILLE: THE PLACE TO EAT T-shirts and holding signs with slogans like, PETERSVILLE: NOT JUST FOR GUYS NAMED PETER and PETERSVILLE: SMALL TOWN VIBE, BIG CITY EATS.

That last one was a stretch, but no more than lots of other ads I'd seen. Besides, since the makeover, Petersville definitely had way more good food than other small towns, so it was true-ish.

Mom even came up with an idea for how we could use the Petersmobile when *Can You Cut It?* was over. It would be like a Petersville food truck, and we'd stock it with local products like popcorn from The Pop Shop and Stinky Cheese Farm cheese, and then drive it to fairs and farmers' markets.

…58…59…

Mom hit the stopwatch. "Time's up."

I groaned. "I got nothing."

"You're trying too hard," she said. "Loosen up. Be creative."

Be creative? That was like saying, "Be smart."

"Can we take a break?"

"No!" Jeanine wagged a Sharpie at me. "Breaks are for krill. Are you krill or are you a shark?"

"Depends. How much sleep do sharks get?"

"That's actually a really interesting question. Scientists don't know whether sharks sleep at all. It has to do with—"

"Jeanine! Do you want me to do this or not?"

"Oh, fine. But you really need to work on your focus."

I squeezed my eyes shut. "Okay, Mexican, Mexican... chicken...avocado?"

"Chicken and avocado? We're talking about *Can You Cut It?* not Chipotle," Jeanine said.

She was right. How much more *blah* could I get? I pressed my palms hard against my closed eyes until I saw purple blobs. "Eggplant?"

"Let's stop." I felt Mom's hands on my shoulders. "You're just fried. Nobody's creative juices flow when they're fried. Besides, I've got to run."

I opened my eyes. "Where?"

Her eyes slid from my face to the floor. "Albany. Zo Zo, go get ready and I'll drop you at Larissa's."

"I am ready." She was wearing bear pajamas.

"Zo Zo, what did we say?"

"We said *clean* clothes. *These* are clean." Zoe pet her furry sleeves.

"You woke up and put on clean pajamas?"

"We did."

Mom looked at her watch, then up at the ceiling, clearly

calculating how much time it would take to argue Zoe out of pajamas. "Fine."

Zoe grinned, poking her tongue through the space where her two front teeth were missing.

"Did we brush our teeth?"

"We didn't."

"Go."

"Bears have teeth and *they* don't brush," Zoe said as she slowly climbed the stairs.

I cleared my bowl and put it in the sink. "So why are you going to Albany?"

"Oh…" She squirted dishwashing liquid onto a sponge. "Walter and I are taking turns going to Albany to pick up food."

"What happened to your suppliers?"

Mom leaned forward and scrubbed hard at a perfectly clean plate with a sponge.

"Mom, what happened to the suppliers?"

"Nothing," she said.

"Mom, I'm not little anymore. I can—"

"Yeah, what's up with that, anyway?" It was Dad, coming down the stairs with his laptop. "There's been all too much growing recently. Cut that out, will you?" He flashed me a goofy smile.

Would it kill them to be straight with me?

"I have to go. Knife skills practice."

"Bye," Dad said.

"See you later," Mom said.

I was at the door when something inside me broke loose, and what I'd been looking for just floated up.

"Hey, Mom," I said, turning back.

"Yeah?"

"Butternut squash, goat cheese tacos with a tomatillo salsa."

"*Woah*. I'd eat that," Mom said.

"Me too," Dad said.

"I hate squash," Zoe said from the top of the stairs where she'd been sitting instead of brushing her teeth.

Maybe I really did stand a chance.

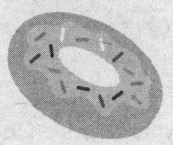
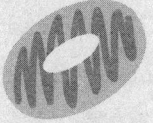

13

The Petersville Gazette

Vol. 1, Issue 11

Vol. 1, Issue 11

Town Happenings

Petersville's First Gamemaker Named: At its last meeting, the Petersville Town Council voted to create the position of Town Gamemaker. The Gamemaker will be charged with designing, scheduling, and running live action games to be held in town. The first Gamemaker will be **Clyde Hammond**, who had this to say: "I'm fired up! The kickoff game will be my own safe-for-all-ages version of *Assassins*. I think people are going to flip for it."

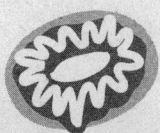

Five brand-new calves born at Stinky Cheese Farm: Owners Riley Carter and June Simms invite anyone and everyone to come visit with Sparky, Spanky, Spartacus, Sprocket, and Spy.

The Petersmobile hits the road: Tris Levin, along with his family, Josh Bell, Mayor Jim Partridge, and Winnie Hammond head out tomorrow for NYC. If you see Tris around town, wish him luck on *Can You Cut It?*!

Featured Series

Things Most People Get Wrong and How YOU Can Get Them Right

By Jeanine Levin

Have your parents ever told you that you can't swim right after you eat? Not true. Studies show that swimming immediately after eating poses no risks. So next time you want to take a dip right after a meal and your parents tell you to wait thirty minutes, give them the facts.

The truth will set you free!

You're welcome!

The ceiling of the Airstream was so close to my face, I had to just lie flat and stare up at it. The thing is: that first night, I wouldn't have been able to sleep even if I had been able to lie on my side with my feet against the wall like I usually do.

The problem was my brain. I couldn't turn it off. I couldn't even slow it down. It was on fast-forward. It was already at tomorrow, at the *Can You Cut It?* studios. It was facing off with Chef JJ and Dieter Koons and those five kids who were going to cook circles around me. It was already busy losing, making mistakes, and forgetting everything. And while it was doing that, it was playing a soundtrack of everyone I was letting down yelling at me.

Mom: *At least two spices per dish, not including salt!*

Zoe: *Don't cry!*

Josh: *Remember the Tea King! Love to compete!*

Winnie: *Tick-tock, watch the clock!*

Walter: *Chop even so it cooks even!*

Dr. C: *It can't just taste good. It's got to look good!*

When I closed my eyes, Jeanine was there, dancing on the insides of my eyelids flinging spatulas like pom-poms and cheering, "Believe and achieve!"

Orange light from the streetlamp filled the Airstream. I'd forgotten how much lighter nighttime is in the city. In Petersville, dark is a can't-see-your-hand-in-front-of-your-face, are-my-eyes-closed-or-open blackness.

We'd had to scratch the plan to keep the Airstream in front of The Food Connection building at night. Parking there during the day wasn't a problem, but a security guard had come out when it started getting dark to tell us we couldn't keep it there overnight. What he actually said was, "This isn't Jabours Motor Lodge." None of us had a clue who Jabours was, but we got the point.

Since my parents knew the guy who owned the lot across from our old building, we drove uptown to camp out there for the night. This meant we'd be able to eat at Barney Greengrass at least once, possibly twice each day. It wouldn't make up for no longer living around the corner from the best deli in the world, but by the time we went back to Petersville, I'd have gotten my fix of eggs and onions, at least for a while.

I know what you're thinking, eggs and onions? How hard can it be to make scrambled eggs with onions? Any old eggs and onions: piece of cake. Barney's eggs and onions, where the eggs are creamy like custard and the onions are so sweet, they taste like they've been cooked with brown sugar: impossible. I've tried. My mother's tried. Walter's tried. They can get close, but it's never exactly right.

Don't believe that any scrambled eggs could be that mind-blowing? Ask Josh. We went to Barney's for dinner after we parked the Airstream, and he tasted them for the first time. I swear he didn't look up from his plate until he'd eaten every last bite, and Josh isn't even an egg fan.

Zippo almost dropped a tray of matzoh ball soups when we came through the door. He rushed over to give us all hugs that smelled like garlic bagels and then had the kitchen make a fresh batch of latkes. Before we moved to Petersville, we saw Zippo every Saturday morning and had for as far back as I could remember.

On our way back to the Petersmobile after dinner, we walked by our old apartment. Zoe wanted to ring the buzzer to see if we could go up, but Mom said we couldn't, so Zoe cried and sat down on the stoop and refused to get up, no matter how many Dessert Days mom threatened to take away. Mom made us all walk away like we were actually going to leave Zoe there, even though everyone, including Zoe, knew we wouldn't.

"What do we do now?" Jim asked when we got to the corner and Zoe was still on the stoop.

"Just wait here and don't turn around," Mom said.

I'm pretty sure Zoe won this round because Mom did eventually turn around and go back for her. Also, because as she was walking back, Zoe ran her hands up and down the whole buzzer panel, ringing every apartment in the building.

I don't think I would have gone up to see our old apartment even if we could have. I'd been looking forward to going back to our old neighborhood, but when we got there, whatever I thought I was going to feel, I didn't. I felt the way I do when I see baby pictures of me, like it's not me, like it's somebody else, somebody I won't ever get to meet and don't even remember but somehow miss. This neighborhood, our old building, none of it was mine anymore.

I lay there staring at the rusty screws in the Airstream ceiling hoping that eventually, when I got tired enough, I'd drift off. But I didn't. I just lay there feeling like a rubber band someone was stretching a little farther every second.

Besides not being that dark, it wasn't that quiet either. You wouldn't think sleeping makes much noise, but the thing about seven people in an RV, really everything they do makes noise, even sleeping.

We were only seven because Dad had gone to G-Mare's—that's what we call his mom—for dinner and decided to stay over. He was the least into the Petersmobile, which wasn't a surprise. He wasn't into much these days, besides his newspaper. He was on his laptop so much, it was basically his new face. Part of me wondered if he even cared if I won *Can You Cut It?* Don't get me wrong. I don't think he wanted me to lose, but that's not the same as wanting me to win. I think what he wanted was for me to want to write dumb articles for his newspaper and go around with a lying, happy face all the time. I guess right now, we both wanted the other one to want something different. And maybe that's okay. What wasn't okay was that I was the only one who could admit it.

Just then, I heard a *scritch-scritch*.

"Shh." It was Zoe. "Go to sleep."

"Zo Zo, who are you talking to?"

She didn't answer. Then there was another *scritch-scritch*, and our bunk bed shook.

I jumped down.

"*Shh!* We're sleeping," Zoe whispered.

I grabbed my phone from my bunk and aimed the light at Zoe. She was on her knees, holding her blanket down over a lump.

"What's under there?"

The lump twitched.

"You didn't."

"He didn't want to stay home all alone."

I ripped off the blanket. There was Henry. "Rabbits don't get lonely."

"Mini lops do!" Zoe stroked Henry's droopy ears.

"Where did you put him when we went to dinner?"

"In his cage. But he wanted to cuddle before bed."

Zoe didn't put up a fight when I told her we had to put Henry back in his cage. She'd either gotten in enough cuddles or was too tired to keep chasing him around the bed.

Before long, she was asleep. I could tell from the way she was breathing. It sounded almost like what you hear when you hold one of those big seashells up to your ear.

"Go to sleep, Slick." Winnie's voice was extra loud and scratchy in the dark.

"How'd you know I was awake?"

"ESP."

"Really?" It would explain a lot if Winnie had the power to read minds.

"No, not really. It's bright as day in here, and your eyes are open." Winnie was in the bunk across from mine. She had some theory that the air would be better on the top.

"I can't stop thinking about tomorrow."

"That helping?"

"What do you mean?"

"I mean, you gonna do better because you stayed up all night stressifying yourself?" This was followed by the sound of Tic Tacs rattling.

Just then, there was a thud and a groan.

"Josh?"

"I was dreaming," Josh said, soft and slow like maybe he wasn't fully awake. "We were at a town meeting and…we were all wearing Chef JJ wigs. Then something happened. I don't remember what. I think that's when I fell out of bed." He pulled his pillow and blanket down onto the floor. "I'm gonna stay down here."

Josh usually sleeps diagonally because he's so tall, but the bunk beds were too narrow for that so he'd hung his legs over the end with his feet resting on the table. Not an easy position to hold in your sleep, I guess.

"Sorry I woke you," Josh whispered.

"You didn't wake anybody." Winnie paused and we could hear the crunching of Tic Tacs. "Slick's planning to stay up all night and work himself up into a lather."

"Work himself into a what?" Josh asked.

"Oh, you know, get good and stressified so he can bomb tomorrow and get kicked off on the first day. Like pulling a Band-Aid off nice and fast, right, Slick?"

"Maybe he's just too excited to sleep," Josh said.

"Is that it, Slick? You excited or stressified? Which one is it?"

"I'm just worried that everything I know about cooking is slipping out of my brain as I lie here."

"That would be stressified then," Winnie said.

"Hey, I have an idea," Josh said. "My mom does this thing if I'm having trouble falling asleep the night before a game. It's going to sound kind of dumb—"

"Fantastic," Winnie said.

"But it works."

"I'll try anything," I said.

"Okay, so close your eyes…"

"Close eyes. Check." The streetlamp was so bright, the insides of my eyelids were orange.

"Picture yourself floating on a lake." Josh was using this voice like Mom uses for Zoe's bedtime story. "The sun's shining down. And the water's the perfect temperature."

"What does that mean?" Winnie said. "The 'perfect' temperature? What's that?"

"It's whatever 'perfect' means to you. That's the point."

"Fine," Winnie said. "I'm floating in the perfect water on the perfect day. This working for you, Slick?"

"I'm not done yet," Josh said. "So now you focus on relaxing each part of your body floating on the water. Start with your toes, think about letting them just float."

I made little fists with my toes, then tried to let go and let them just float. But they wouldn't. The more I told them to relax, the heavier they got, the more they pulled me down. My toes were so heavy, they were going to drown me.

"Okay, now your ankles…"

When Josh was done, every part of my body had sunk to the bottom of that lake where it was dark and cold. Winnie was snoring.

"Isn't that cool?" Josh said. "It always works for me."

"Uh-huh. Thanks." It wasn't Josh's fault I was too stressified to float.

"You think you can sleep now?"

"Oh, yeah," I lied.

Then I lay there at the bottom of the lake waiting for morning.

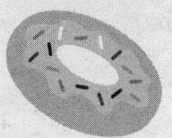

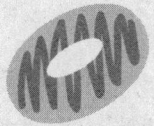

14

Winnie cut a sharp right out of Central Park onto Fifth Avenue, and I grabbed onto one of the bunk bed chains to keep from flying across the Airstream. "What's the rush? I don't have to be there until nine." It was so early, the streetlights were still lit.

Winnie swerved around a delivery truck. "We gotta be parked out front for *Breakfast with Brit*."

"I think her name is Brynn," Mom said. She was still in bed. Zoe had somehow squeezed in there with her during the night and was asleep, curled in a ball, her butt in the air.

"What's *Breakfast with Brynn*?" I said.

"Oh, my mom loves that show!" Josh called from the bathroom.

"You know." Jeanine sat up in her bunk. "That show with the

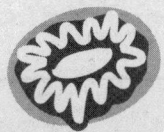

lady in the bed they roll out onto the street. Sometimes they show ads for it during *Can You Cut It?*"

"Oh, right. People really watch that?"

"Oh, yeah." Josh opened the bathroom door holding his toothbrush. "It's kind of weird. She has guests come on in their pajamas, and they make breakfast together, and eat it in this big bed."

"So why do we care about *Breakfast with Brynn*?" I said.

"Renny says people love her!" Jim called from the passenger seat.

"I still don't get it. What does this have to do with us?"

Josh, mid-tooth brushing, held up a finger, then spat into the tiny sink. "All her fans, they line up on the sidewalk in front of the building every morning because she comes out there with her bed and her cameras and talks to people. My mom had this idea that if we were standing out there in front of the Petersmobile, you know, in our T-shirts with our signs, we could get her to talk to us on air. Talk about buzz, right?"

Winnie stopped short, and we all jerked forward. "Will you look at those boneheads," she said. "Don't they have anything better to do? I mean, we're here trying to save a town. They're just...wasting their lives."

Police barricades ran across the plaza, and behind them stood a crowd of maybe forty or so people, many holding signs saying stuff like, "We love you Brynn," and "Came from New Orleans to have breakfast with Brynn."

Josh stooped down to get a better look out the window. "Are they wearing pajamas?"

"Oh, yeah," I said. "Way too many polka dots and team logos for regular clothing."

"Look at that lady with the huge Elmo slippers." Jeanine pointed.

"All right, everybody. Time to suit up." Jim popped open a panel, pulled out a bag, and began handing out T-shirts.

The Petersmobile was a hit. Not with the *Breakfast with Brynn* fans. They were too busy trying to make sure they were up front when Brynn came out. Most of the people rushing to work also didn't give us a second look. So who were all those people taking selfies with the Petersmobile and Zoe and Henry? Tourists. Summer in midtown Manhattan is packed with tourists— hopefully tourists who were going to make Petersville their next destination.

About a quarter to nine, a bunch of guys in black T-shirts and pants rolled Brynn's enormous bed out of the building into the plaza.

The crowd went crazy, yelling and screaming and shaking signs even though there wasn't a camera in sight.

"We should go," I said to Mom.

"Too bad Brynn and her cameras aren't here yet," Josh said.

"I think being late would be bad." I handed him my sign.

"Break a leg," Jim said. "Does that work for a cooking show? Or is that just for regular shows?"

"You want him to waste time with stupid questions or you want him to go win some cash?" Winnie pulled me in close. "Good luck, Slick."

"Thanks," I said.

"Don't forget," Jeanine said.

"I know. I know. Believe and achieve."

Mom and I signed in with lobby security, then headed for the elevators.

As we zoomed up, Mom studied herself in the mirrored doors.

"Oh, boy." She combed her fingers through her hair, then squinted and pointed at the me in the doors. "Is that toothpaste?" She licked a finger and came at the real me with it.

I held up a hand to block her. "Hey, we talked about this. Saliva is not a cleaning product."

Using the doors as a mirror, I rubbed the mint green stain off my chin with the back of my hand.

"Sorry. I think I'm just a little nervous about seeing JJ after so long," she admitted to the us in the doors.

That's when I realized something, something I should have realized the moment I'd heard I'd gotten on the show: everyone was going to find out that Mom and Chef JJ worked together, and after that, it wouldn't matter how good my skills were, they'd never believe I deserved to be there. They'd think that I was chosen because Chef JJ was friends with my mom.

The elevator *pinged* to a stop. No time to think about this now, not that I could do anything about it anyway. The doors slid open.

"Here we go." I stepped off the elevator.

"Tristan?" A woman with hair dyed the color of a pearl was walking toward us across a hall of elevators. She wore a headset attached to a walkie-talkie and was holding a clipboard.

"Hi. It's Tris, actually."

"Oh, Tris, right," she said super slowly, like she couldn't care less and wanted me to know it. "I'm Randy. You'll see a lot of me because I'm the assistant producer responsible for all you contestants. I'm really looking forward to getting to know all of you." This last part sounded like she was reading off her clipboard. "This is the schedule." She handed me a sheet of paper. "Of course, it will depend on what happens in the competition."

She might as well have said, "Like if you choke, you don't need this at all."

"So here's the plan. First, we'll take you through to hair and makeup—"

"Makeup?"

"We're not talking beauty pageant makeup. They just make sure you won't look washed out on camera from all the lights."

Randy kept talking as she led us through a maze of hallways into a room full of mirrors and people standing around staring at their phones.

"Where are the other kids?" I asked.

"They're done."

"Already?" I looked at my phone. Just one minute after nine.

"Yeah, most of them got here around eight. I guess they were just super excited."

Was this Randy's way of saying that *I* must not be super excited because I came at the time they told me to?

"Oh, I'll take that." Randy snatched my phone out of my hand. "You can get it back after taping each day."

"Terrence!"

A tall, thin guy with a headset stretched over a mountain of dreadlocks ran over.

"This is Terrence." Randy handed him my phone. "He's our PA in charge of the contestants."

"PA?" I said.

"Production assistant," Terrence explained. "Welcome to the show."

"Thanks."

Next thing I knew, Terrence whisked me into a chair in front of a mirror so bright, it was like staring into the sun.

For the next half hour, I was poked, sprayed, creamed, and powdered. A lady wearing hairbrushes on a tool belt even cut my hair. She claimed she had to because you couldn't see my face, but since she basically gave me a whole new haircut, I wasn't buying it.

Then, as if that wasn't enough, they made me lift up my T-shirt so they could stick a tiny microphone to my bare chest.

When I was finally allowed to stand up, some guy came over to examine all my clothing for logos, you know, like the Nike swoosh. He tried to explain why. I didn't get everything, but the bottom line is, it's against the law to show logos on TV unless the company that owns the logo says it's okay.

Once logo guy cleared me, Randy explained that I'd be going to the greenroom and Mom would be headed to the parents' lounge where she could watch the filming on a live feed.

"What's the greenroom?" I asked, trying to keep up with Randy as she speed-walked down another long hallway.

"Where you'll be before the segments. It's like a hangout room."

When we got to the door of the parents' lounge, Mom took my chin in her hand and looked right into my eyes. "You got this. You're going to be great." There was something about the way she said it that made me feel like she was trying to cast a spell, like by saying it she could make it come true.

"See you after," I said, and hurried to catch up with Randy who was already on the move.

"And this is you…" Randy opened a heavy metal door marked GREENROOM. "Everyone, meet Tris."

Everyone, three girls and two boys, looked up from different spots in the room.

"We still have a while before we go to set. So just relax. Have something to eat." She waved her clipboard in the direction of a table piled high with food. "I'll see you in a bit." Then she sped off.

For a second, I just stood there, trying to figure out where to park myself. Maybe behind one of the many potted trees scattered around the room. I was under orders from Jeanine not to talk to the competition any more than necessary.

I wasn't there to make friends. I was there to win. No chatting with the enemy. Jeanine had given strict instructions. I was supposed to tune everyone out.

I hate the competition. I love to compete…

A girl on one of the couches raised a plastic knife covered with cream cheese and pointed it at me. "Hey, I remember you. Doughnuts, right?"

The trash-talker. Of course she'd made it. "Uh, yeah."

She whistled. "Those must have been some doughnuts."

They were. Even if Chef JJ never bothered to find out.

"You got on with *doughnuts*?" said a boy circling the food table. He looked about my age and was all in black, right down to his skinny jeans. He forced a laugh. "Let me guess, you called them *beignets*."

"What are *beignets*?" a boy sprawled across one of the armchairs asked.

"*Beignet* is just fancy for doughnut," Trash-talker said.

"It's actually French for doughnut," Skinny Jeans said.

"Who cares what you call them? I love doughnuts," the boy on the armchair said before biting into a muffin. He was definitely younger than me. He reminded me of Riley's new puppy, same gold-red hair, same hands and feet (or in Fozzie's case, paws) that were way too big for their bodies.

Without thinking, I headed for the food table. At least eating was something to do besides letting people psych me out.

"Are we supposed to know that?" A small girl popped out from behind the table. She looked like a living, breathing Disney character, with huge brown eyes, pink-pink cheeks, and sleek black pigtails.

"Know what?" Trash-talker asked.

"Names for food in French," the girl said.

"You mean, you *don't*?" Skinny Jeans said.

The girl's eyes grew even bigger. "That's not fair. That's not even… I mean, why French? Why do people always think French food is so great? Have you ever had *sata andagi*? I bet they're way better than French doughnuts."

"*Woah.*" Trash-talker put her hands up like she was surrendering. "Relax. First of all, he's messing with you. Second of all, what are *sata andagi*?"

"Okinawan doughnuts."

"Cool." Trash-talker picked up her jacket from the couch—the one she'd been wearing at the callback with all the buttons—and pulled out a tiny notebook and pen. "So I can just call them Okinawan doughnuts?"

"What are you doing?" the girl asked.

"I write down foods I want to try in here, so I don't forget. You think if I just google 'Okinawan doughnuts,' I'll be able to find places that serve them?"

"I guess."

I should get a notebook like that, I thought. Or maybe I could just use my phone. Could I hate Trash-talker and be impressed by her at the same time?

"And you're sure he was just…messing with me, you know, about the French?" the Disney character asked.

"Yeah, I'm sure. I'm pretty sure that's his job."

"No, it's not," Skinny Jeans snapped. "Wait, what do you mean, my job?"

Trash-talker rolled her eyes. "I *mean*, that's why you were chosen. Because they thought you'd mess with people. You don't think this show is all about cooking, do you? They want drama— you know, fights and tears and freak-outs. What did you think all those questions—winning is everything—were all about?"

The room went silent.

I wondered what kind of drama they thought I'd bring. What was I picked for: tears, fights, or freak-outs?

I grabbed a plate and circled the food table slowly. They had everything: bagels, cream cheese, cubed cheese, mini muffins, egg sandwiches, cut fruit. I guess it made sense that The Food Connection put out a good spread.

I hadn't had a decent bagel in forever, and these looked like they didn't come from bags in the freezer. They were nice and plump. I was just reaching for an egg one when I felt someone tap me on the shoulder.

I jerked away and looked up.

It was a girl. She was smiling and holding out bagel tongs.

I took the tongs, mumbled a thanks, and tried to glue my eyes to my bagel, but the more I tried not to see that girl, the more she was all I could see. Her face was red-brown like Mom's herb pots, and her dark hair was twisted up on either side of her head like Princess Leia in that old Star Wars movie.

And she was still smiling.

If trash-talking was bad for your competitive edge, smiling was like dynamite.

"The bagels are really good." She sounded like she'd just walked out of Hogwarts. She wasn't from the East Coast. She didn't even sound like she was from this country. "This is my second. I like the egg ones too. I'm Keya."

"Hey." I grabbed a handful of mini muffins, slapped some cream cheese onto my plate, and went in search of a chair as far away as possible.

Eating was the perfect activity. It gave me something to do, and it made me feel good.

On the couch opposite me, Skinny Jeans was twirling a quarter between his fingers. I tried to focus on the mountain of food on the plate in my lap, but something kept pulling my eyes to his face.

"Problem?" he said.

"Uh, me?"

"Yeah, you." And that's when I realized what it was. His eyebrow. The left one. Half of it was missing. "Do you, like, need something? Because you're creeping me out."

"No, no. Sorry." I forced my eyes to my half-eaten bagel.

I couldn't look at anyone. I wasn't supposed to talk to anyone. Fine. I'd eat.

Before I knew it, I'd cleaned the entire plate. I'd basically inhaled it, and the second it was gone, I missed the activity: *put food in mouth, chew, swallow, repeat*. And in between, there was that little burst of happy from my taste buds.

So I went for seconds.

And thirds.

Four mini waffles, two bagels, an egg sandwich, half a mango, and one cheese Danish later, Randy was back, clapping her hands. "Okay, people. Now, rules, rules, rules." She handed each of us a piece of a paper. "When the show is over, or is over for you, you must return these to me. You may not copy these rules or share them with anyone else. If these rules end up in the public or on the internet, you will be immediately cut from the show and the show's lawyers will come after your family for everything they own. Got it? Just kidding about the lawyers. Totally serious about kicking you off though."

Just then, something came to life in the pit of my stomach, something angry and loud, a creature made of all the food I'd just packed into me. I leaned back to give it space to stretch out but all that did was allow it to reach up into my chest and squeeze my heart.

Randy returned to the center of the room and made another violent check on her clipboard. "Now, we will go through the rules." She sounded like those safety videos on airplanes. "Rule Number One: no touching Chef JJ. Not once, not ever."

Got it. No touching Chef JJ. Check. Check. Double-check.

Somebody laughed.

"Don't laugh." Randy clicked her pen in and out. "The rules are not funny."

The younger boy burst out laughing, then slapped his hands over his mouth.

"I'm… It's just, why would we touch her?" It was Keya, that girl who sounded like Hermione.

Randy glared. "I'm saying, don't shake her hand or high-five her. Chef JJ doesn't do that. Got it?"

"Got it," Keya said, but you could tell she still thought it was funny.

Just then, I felt a cramp like the monster was standing on a major organ, and I stretched out even farther, so far now that my butt was barely on the seat.

"Rule Number Two: eyes on Chef JJ or Dieter or your station only. No looking off camera."

"How come?" asked the Disney character.

"Because it's obnoxious. Moving on." Randy made another angry check.

"Why is it obnoxious?"

Randy took a deep breath and exhaled hard like she was the wolf trying to blow down one of the little pigs' houses.

"Because," Skinny Jeans said, "nobody wants to watch a show where the people on the screen are looking at something they can't see."

Right then, the beast in my stomach shook its cage so hard you could hear the bars rattle.

Randy's head jerked up from her clipboard. She scanned the room, but the monster was taking a break. "Rule Number Three," she continued, still eyeing the room, "if someone gets hurt, call for the medic. We have one on set at all times. So, kids, if you find yourself in need of medical assistance, you yell..."

Nobody said anything.

"You yell..." Randy waved a hand as if she was conducting an orchestra.

"Medic," we repeated.

"Bravo."

"Okay, that's it." *Click. Click. Check.* "Any questions?"

That's when the beast delivered a punch that sent me flying out of my chair.

Randy aimed her pen right at me. *Click. Click.* "You okay?"

"Yeah, just a...cramp."

"You sure? You're, like, green."

"Oh, um, that's just me."

"I don't think so. People who are green normally are like, olive. You're a whole different green." Then she clicked a button on her walkie, pulled the mic on her headset down to her mouth, and said, "Randy to Terrence, what's your twenty? Okay... When you're done there, I need you to get one of those alternates to come in. Like, now." Her eyes yo-yoed up and down me.

"No!" I lunged forward and felt the monster slosh against the sides of my stomach.

"Hey, relax," Randy ordered, holding her pen out like a

wand. "If you're fine, no worries. We just have to cover our you-know-whats."

"Okay, because I *am* fine. I really am always this color. I get it from my dad."

The truth was, I was not at all fine.

The truth was, I wanted to lie on the floor and not move for a very long time, but I wasn't going to lose this thing before I'd even started. How would I ever be able to face anyone if I'd failed because I'd eaten myself sick? What kind of nuddy eats like Joey Chestnut, world-famous competitive eater, right before the first round of *Can You Cut It?*

"Really, I'm good."

Randy so wasn't buying the all-the-men-in-my-family-are-green excuse. She held her hand over her headset mouthpiece and glared at me. "You get that you can't be sick, right? No sickness allowed."

"Is that a rule too?" Skinny Jeans asked. "Because it's not on the sheet."

"Yeah, it's a rule, but someone in legal said we couldn't write that one down. But just so you know, it is. No sickness allowed on the show. Not a fever. Not a cold. Not even a sneeze. You got me?"

I nodded slowly so as not to disturb the beast even though

what I was thinking was, nobody ever sneezes? Really? Didn't you explode if you tried to hold in a sneeze?

Randy uncovered her mic. "Randy to Terrence…yeah, just keep the alternate on standby until further notice… No, the kid says he's, like, related to Kermit the Frog… Yeah, totally green… He knows, he knows." Then she pushed a button on the walkie and bent the mic away from her face. "Okay, people, line up."

Everyone except me raced to the door.

"*Woah!*" Randy shooed everybody back with her clipboard.

I walked slowly across the room and took my place at the back of the line. *I'm fine. I'm fine.*

In front of me, Keya turned around. "Maybe you could ask the medic for a Paracetamol," she said quietly.

"What?"

"Oh, sorry—I meant a Tylenol."

Why couldn't this girl mind her own business? "I don't need anything. We should go." Randy had already led the group out of the room, and I slipped around Keya to catch up with them.

I was fine. I was. Believe and achieve, right?

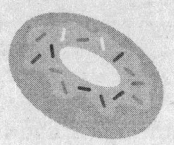

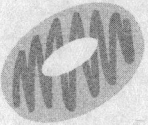

15

"Listen up, I'm going to call your name, then tell you which counter you're assigned to."

I blinked against the lights. They were everywhere.

And how many cameras did they need? I counted two enormous ones on wheels that looked like Transformers at the front of the set, and six smaller ones that people were holding on their shoulders at each end of three long counters.

"There are two of you to a counter." Randy held up two fingers like maybe we needed a visual aid to understand the number two.

"Izzy?"

"Here!" The Disney character's arm shot in the air.

Randy waved her forward. "You too, Harper."

Trash-talker joined Izzy. I noticed she'd put on her jean jacket

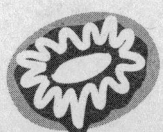

even though it was superhot from all the lights, and I wondered whether it was some good luck thing.

"So you two are together at station one."

A woman in green hospital scrubs with a gummy smile waved from the first counter.

"Guys, that's April. She's the medic." Randy looked at her clipboard. "Okay, next up… Phoenix?" Skinny Jeans raised his hand. "And Gordy?"

The boy who reminded me of Fozzie pumped his fist in the air. "Can you cut it!" he called like he was leading a cheer at the Super Bowl.

"You two are together."

"Excellent." Phoenix rolled his eyes. "When does Chef JJ get here?"

"When you do what I tell you to. Now go to your station." Randy clicked her pen over her head like she was firing warning shots.

Phoenix made a face and dragged his feet over to his counter where Gordy was already bouncing around touching all the equipment.

"So that leaves…" Randy clicked her pen at Keya.

"Keya," the girl said.

"Keya, right. You're with Tristan—Tris."

"Hello, again," Keya said to me.

"Hey." I felt my mouth break into a smile against my will. Not smiling at Keya while she was smiling at me was like trying to sing "The Star-Spangled Banner" in a stadium full of people singing "Happy Birthday."

Why couldn't I have been with Phoenix, someone I could hate and who would hate me right back?

We followed Randy to our counter where someone was squatting in front of the shelves under it, checking things off on an iPad.

"*This* is Marco." The man stood up, and I recognized him as the guy who'd interviewed me at the callback. "Marco is an assistant producer. His job is to... he helps keep the show exciting." Randy's face broke into a smile, a real one with teeth. "And we don't know what we'd do without him."

"Stop or you'll make me tear up in front of the kids." Marco gave Randy a one-armed hug. "So, who are the latest victims?"

Randy introduced Marco to everyone, then took us through the day's filming schedule. Since Chef JJ shot the intro to the show separately, she and Dieter would jump right in with introducing us and then go straight into the first challenge.

"What else? What am I forgetting?" Randy flipped through papers on her clipboard. "Oh, right, interviews! Over the course of the show, we'll be pulling you aside and interviewing you individually. Given the way the show works, sometimes the interviews happen after you've been cut. We know these can be hard, but we'll try to make them fast so you can get out of here."

Just then, the woman with the toothpaste commercial smile I remembered from the callback rushed onto the set and whispered something to Randy.

"Okay, everybody. This is it!" Randy called.

Seconds later, Chef JJ walked out of the camera lights onto the set.

For a moment, everyone, camerapeople unspooling cable, kids checking out their equipment, people adjusting lights, stopped what they were doing.

Chef JJ gave a round-the-room wave. She was wearing a leather vest over the whitest T-shirt I'd ever seen, so white and clean, it was like she was daring us to spill something on it.

"And we're off." Marco jogged to the front of the set. "All right, everybody excited?"

We all "yeah-ed."

"That doesn't sound very excited," Marco said. "Let's try that again. Everybody excited?" He cupped a hand over an ear.

We "yeah-ed" louder.

I felt like I was at a first-grade birthday party.

While Marco was pumping us up, three guys wearing enormous earphones and carrying long poles with microphones attached to the ends positioned themselves around the room, two on opposite ends of the set, and one next to Chef JJ.

"Thanks, Marco," Chef JJ said. "Now *I'm* excited. You guys are going to rock this challenge. Just remember!" She pointed to the tattoo on her arm. "Never..."

"Give up!" we all shouted. Marco had done his job well.

"Hello, hello, hello!" sang Dieter as he walked out of the camera lights wearing a suit the color of Astroturf.

"Okay, guys, one last thing," Randy called. "Marco will be running on and off set. Don't worry. He gets edited out, but the cameras are always rolling. Take it away, Samara."

Samara, all toothpaste smiles, ran out from behind the cameras with a mini chalkboard and held it up in front of her. "*Can You Cut It?* Season 6, Take 1." Then she clapped down a lever on the board with a loud snap, and we were off.

Chef JJ and Dieter crossed the set to Izzy and Harper's counter trailed by a woman piloting the Transformer camera and a guy suspending the pole with the microphone over their heads.

"So, why don't you tell us a little bit about yourself?" Chef JJ said to Izzy.

"I'm Izzy Ban-Newton. I'm from Portland, Maine. I'm eight years old."

"Okay, Izzy, and how long have you been cooking?"

"Since I was four."

"And did I hear you've got some kind of cooking business?"

"Oh, yeah. Lunchbox. Parents hire me to make healthy bento box lunches for their kids and then they pick them up from me and Mom before school."

"Well, isn't that so...useful?"

"Very useful." Dieter nodded.

"And, Izzy, what's your favorite dish to make?"

"Oh..." Izzy twirled a finger in a pigtail.

"*Tick-tock*," Dieter sang.

"Pie?" Izzy said.

"Pie, huh? Good pie takes real skill. You know why, right?" Chef JJ asked.

"Um..." Izzy chewed on a thumbnail.

This was one question I could answer even before I started training for the show. It's the crust. Fillings are easy. But to make a crust that's perfectly flaky, you have to know what you're doing. The trick is cold butter. I've started putting the whole pie in the freezer for a bit right before I pop it in the oven. Works like a charm.

"Maybe taste the fruit before so you know how much sugar you need?" Izzy said.

"Come on, Izzy. Any kid with a subscription to *Cooks Illustrated* knows that."

Izzy's chin quivered.

I was beginning to understand what Izzy's role was. She was the one you were supposed to feel bad for. She was there for the *aww* effect.

"What about you?" Chef JJ crossed from Izzy's station to Harper's. "You are?"

"Harper Gonzalez, thirteen."

"And do you, Harper Gonzalez, thirteen, know why pie takes real skill?"

"The crust. Most people's crust tastes… Well, it's really bad."

"Too true," Dieter said.

"So, what's the secret?" Chef JJ asked.

"Butter. It's got to be cold."

Chef JJ nodded. "Exactly. Gold star for Ms. Gonzalez. And how did you learn to cook?"

"My parents. They met at the French Culinary Institute, and now they own a food truck in Philly."

"Food truck, huh?" Chef JJ rubbed her arms like the thought gave her the chills. "What kind of food?"

"Chinese. Szechuan," Harper said.

"And they've never wanted to own a real restaurant?"

Harper pressed her lips together as if she were trying to keep something dangerous from popping out. "I think they think it's plenty real."

"I guess it's all a matter of perspective, right?" Chef JJ said, giving Harper an icy smile.

Next up was Phoenix. He was twelve, from Vermont, had five brothers, and they were all homeschooled.

"And do I have this right," Chef JJ said, "two of your brothers are on the Junior Olympic ski team, two are on the junior national speed skating team, and the youngest is a world-class... What was it?"

"Snowboarder," Phoenix said. "Yeah, that's right."

"What are they putting in the water at your house?" Dieter chuckled.

"And do you ski or skate?" Chef JJ asked.

"Neither."

"Snowboard?"

"Nope."

"Because you cook? That's *your* thing?"

"Yeah." One of Phoenix's eyes twitched.

"And now you want to show them that you're the national cooking champion, yes?" Dieter said.

Phoenix nodded.

"Okay, Phoenix." Chef JJ leaned in a little closer. "I don't want to embarrass you, but I have to ask. What happened to your eyebrow?"

Phoenix's eye did a double-twitch. "It was just, you know, a joke. My, uh, two of my brothers shaved off half of it while I was sleeping."

"Big families. So fun," Dieter said.

"Yeah, it's great." Phoenix looked like he wanted to throw something.

Whatever role Phoenix was supposed to play, I felt like they'd just wound him up to play it.

After Phoenix came Gordy, the puppy. They spent the shortest time with him. Basically the only thing I learned was that he was ten, lived in Delaware, and learned to cook because he loved to eat.

Then I was up.

"You're here. That's so *fabulous*," Chef JJ said in a way that made "fabulous" sound like the scariest three syllables on Earth. "Dieter, did I tell you Tristan's mother and I worked together?"

I flinched at her use of "Tristan" instead of "Tris" but kept silent.

"Yes, I know," Dieter said.

And now everybody else did too.

Phoenix and Harper were glaring at me already.

"Is Mom here?" It felt like Chef JJ was speaking especially loudly.

"Uh, yeah. My whole family."

"Oh, big fun," Dieter said.

"Can't *wait* to see her later. So, *Tristan*…" Chef JJ paused, and winked at me—was she calling me Tristan just to annoy me? "Tell us a little about yourself."

"And maybe too, what means 'Petersville, The Place to Eat,'" Dieter said, pointing at my shirt.

This was it, possibly my only chance to plug Petersville. I took a deep breath. *Go slow. Don't forget anything.* "I'm *Tris* Levin. I'm twelve. And I'm from Petersville, which is in upstate New York, only a short car ride from New York City, Albany, and Boston. It's a beautiful spot surrounded by mountains and farmland. And Petersville is the best small-town destination for food in the country. You get a real small town feel and top-notch cuisine at The Station House and life-changing doughnuts at my doughnut shop, The Doughnut Stop. There's also a local cheese maker, local organic popcorn. Plus, tons of scheduled family activities in town." I'd pointed out to Jeanine that not all of my speech was technically true, but she said we had to fake it till we made it.

"Petersville, huh? Life-changing doughnuts, top-notch cuisine, and beautiful countryside. Sounds intriguing. Maybe we should check it out," Chef JJ said to Dieter.

"Yes, yes. I love the road-tripping."

No way. Had Chef JJ actually said "Petersville" on camera?

Get Chef JJ to say "Petersville." Check. And it was only day one. Plus, she and Dieter were going to visit. How many people would come to Petersville just because Chef JJ said she was planning to go even if she never actually did?

"The whole town would flip for that," I said. "I mean, the whole town isn't that many people, but still."

"So it is a very small place?" Dieter said.

"Oh, yeah. But we're working on growing, you know, getting more people to visit, maybe even move there. I don't know if you know about this, I mean, I didn't, but some upstate New York towns are in big trouble. People are moving away, and the towns are just disappearing."

"I have actually heard about this, Tris," Chef JJ said. "And here's what I have to say about it: survival of the fittest."

"You mean, like, what's it called, natural selection?" We'd learned about that in fifth-grade science. What did animals adapting to their environment over millions of years have to do with Petersville?

"Exactly." Chef JJ snapped her fingers. "*I* think what's happening with these towns can be explained by Darwin's theory of natural selection. Now he was talking about animals, right? But it works here too. Places that don't have the traits that allow them to survive get smaller and smaller until they die out altogether. That's how evolution works. But I guess keeping a few around like museums makes sense. Kind of like the way we breed animals on the verge of extinction in zoos." Chef JJ stroked her bare skull. "Anyway, moving on…"

Had Chef JJ just said that Petersville deserved to die out like the dinosaurs?

Was that what she actually thought or was she just trying to wind me up too?

The next thing I knew, someone was shouting: "CUT!"

The show was deadly serious about giving us breaks, standardized-test-put-your-pencils-down-now serious. Between you and me, I don't think anybody actually cared whether we had to go to the bathroom or were hungry, but it turns out there are laws about the care and feeding of kids when you're making money off us. So we were hustled to the greenroom for exactly fifteen minutes—they set an alarm—and then hustled back to the set where Chef JJ, Dieter, and Marco were waiting for us.

Marco pumped us up for a few minutes (*Who here has mad cooking skills? Let me hear you say, "Yayuh!"*) and then *snap*, the cameras were rolling.

"This is it. The first challenge. Do you think they're ready, Dieter?" Chef JJ said.

Dieter pulled his 3-D glasses down his nose and looked around the room. "They look ready."

"Okay, then. Here it is. Your first challenge is," Chef JJ paused. "Knife Skills Showdown!"

Of course. Because why not get eliminated in the very first round. They couldn't have started with a bake-off?

"Now, as most of you know, Knife Skills Showdown is a challenge in every season, and that's because it tests one of the most fundamental skills we chefs need. It immediately separates the weak from the strong. If you can't cut, you'll never cut it. Each of you has three onions in the cupboard under your sink. Take them out now."

I reached down, pulled my bag of onions out, and dumped it upside down. Three very large onions rolled out.

Two of Keya's onions could have fit inside one of mine. I checked out everybody else's. There were a range of sizes, but nobody's largest onion was close to as big as my smallest.

"Do you think somebody injected your onions with human growth hormone?" Keya said. "You should say something."

"It's fine."

It wasn't. I barely had a fighting chance with normal-size onions, but the few times I'd seen a kid work up the nerve to complain about anything on *Can You Cut It?* Chef JJ tormented and mocked them for being weak for the rest of the show.

"Now, when I start this stopwatch." She held up a large digital clock. "The timers on your counters will also start. There's no time limit on this challenge. Just chop each onion into even pieces as fast as possible. You will be judged on both speed and precision. If you finish first, but I find one strip of half-cut onions, you won't win. You have to find that perfect balance between speed and accuracy."

"And safety," Dieter added.

"Right. Get blood on your onion and you're out. Now review your equipment and make sure you're not missing anything."

Three humungous onions: check.

Knife rack: check.

I looked up and waited for the next instructions.

Beside me, Keya slid a leather envelope onto the counter and unfolded it. Inside, four knives were nestled in leather pouches, each with a sleek pearly handle.

She had her own knives? Nobody had brought their own knives since Parker in Season Two.

Keya wrapped her hand around the largest handle, slid the knife out of its pocket, and held it up to the light. I must have been staring because she smiled that freakishly friendly smile right at me and said, "My father made them for me."

"Cool," I heard myself say.

Not only were they hers, the knives had been specially *made* for her! Next, she was going to tell me they had dragon heartstring cores.

I grabbed the largest plastic handle sticking out of my rack and pulled. The knife was nothing special, but it had a short wide blade that Walter had assured me gave good control.

So she had her own knives, so what.

All I had to do was not finish last.

"Okay, folks, this is it. Knife Skills Showdown!" Chef JJ shouted. "No way to fake knife skills. If you can't cut, you're in trouble starting now!"

The clock on our counter began counting off seconds in glowing red numbers.

Dieter blew a kazoo. "Go and go and go!"

I unraveled three paper towels from the roll next to the sink, ripped them off, wet them, and lay them under the cutting board—a trick Walter had taught me to keep the board stable.

I might not be the fastest chopper, but I knew what I was doing.

I sliced off the tip of an onion, and put it flat side down on the board so it wouldn't roll. I cut it in half and pulled off the peel. Then I pressed my left hand flat on the top of one half and made two horizontal cuts.

Kashish, kashish, kashish.

Before I could stop them, my eyes jumped to Keya's board. With every *kashish* of her blade, a mound of perfectly formed rectangular bits tumbled onto the cutting board. And just like that, she was done with her first onion.

01:01…01:02…

I had to get moving.

I turned my onion and started vertical cuts across the surface.

What was I doing? The cuts were ugly, uneven. Jeez, I hoped Walter wouldn't get to see a close-up of this.

I tried not to think about anybody else, but Keya's *kashish, kashish, kashish* was impossible to shut out.

"Look at her go!" It was Chef JJ. Out of the corner of my eye, I could see her and Dieter at the end of our counter.

01:52…01:53…

I started on my second onion.

"And would you look at those pieces, like a machine cut them."

They were definitely not talking about my chopped onion.

Just then, there was a loud clatter.

We all stopped and looked around.

At the second counter, Gordy stood with his long arms up over his head like he was surrendering, and both he and Phoenix were staring at something on the floor between them.

"How do you drop a knife?" Phoenix said. "You could have killed me."

"I'm really sorry." Gordy's hands were shaking.

"Don't just stand there. Pick it up!" Chef JJ shouted. "And why have the rest of you stopped?"

"*Tick-tock. Tick-tock,*" Dieter said.

02:28…02:29…

This was it, my chance! All I had to do now was not drop the knife. It wouldn't matter how messed up my cuts were. You drop the knife, you're automatically last.

Don't drop the knife. Don't drop the knife. Don't drop the knife…

I used the words to shut everyone else out and keep my rhythm.

Don't (chop)…drop (chop)…the (chop)…knife (chop)….

As I made the last slice, I heard Dieter sing, "Don't drop the knife" right along with me, then laughter.

No, no, no. Had I been saying the words out loud?

I looked up. Everyone's eyes were on me.

"Way to set the bar high," Chef JJ sneered. "But so we're clear, just because you can hold on to your knife, doesn't mean you know how to use it. You got lucky."

"CUT!"

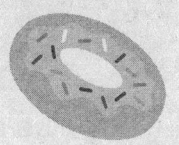

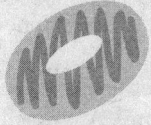

16

Interview with Phoenix Carter, Age 12, Middlebury, Vermont:

You want to know how I'm feeling? I don't think it's fair that girl—Keya, right?—brought her own knives. I mean, did you, like, inspect them? I seriously hope so, because they could have been...I don't know, like, not regulation. They inspect footballs at the Super Bowl, right? Isn't it, like, the same thing? I still came in second with the regular knives, so I probably would have won with her special ones. I mean, it's not as if I care. As long as you don't get eliminated, what difference does it make? You just need to be the last one standing.

Still, it's kind of bogus, you know, using your

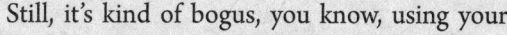

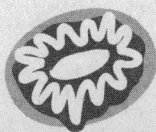

own knives. And they weren't just normal knives from home. Her dad made them for her. Plus, she was telling us he's an engineer. Her knives were, like, specifically designed for her hand. Anyway, I'm over it.

Mom must have said how great I was five times before we even left the parents' lounge, which was annoying both because I just wanted to get out of there and because she knew as well as I did, it wasn't true. I'd gotten lucky, just like Chef JJ said.

Mom was still pulling her stuff together when the lounge door swung open.

"Kira!" Chef JJ called from clear across the room.

All conversation immediately stopped.

Out of the corner of my eye, I saw Harper do a double-take. She and the other contestants and their families were still there.

"JJ, what's it been, like fifteen years?" Mom walked forward, arms open.

"Way too long," Chef JJ said, blocking Mom's hug with a two-handed wave. "So, this handsome boy is yours, I hear."

Something about Chef JJ calling me "h-a-n-d-s-o-m-e" made me feel like there were spiders crawling all over me.

"Guilty as charged." Mom mussed my hair. "Handsome *and* talented."

Melt me, please melt me into a pool of water on the floor.

"But needs some work on those knife skills, am I right? Like mother, like son, I guess. What *was* it Romero was always saying about the way you held a knife?"

Mom's face went tight.

"Tris is a phenomenal cook. He's going to knock your socks off." Mom thumped me on the back, and I know it was supposed to be a you'll-get-'em-next-time thump, but it was weirdly hard and stung.

"Can't. Wait," Chef JJ said, and for a split second, I could have sworn I saw her ice-blue eyes lasering into my mother like she was a contestant on the show.

To celebrate my not getting cut on the very first day, Mom, Dad, Jim, Winnie, Josh, Zoe, Jeanine, and I all went out for dim sum.

Good Chinese is hard to come by upstate, so when we're back in the city, we eat as much of it as we can. I didn't feel like celebrating, but I'm always up for Nom Wah.

It was dark when we climbed out of the subway station in Chinatown, but even without the sun beating down, it was still hot. The air was heavy and wet, and smelled of the garbage rotting in the bags piled on the sidewalk.

The streets were narrow and crowded so we walked single file with Dad leading the way.

A block from the restaurant, we hit a crowd of shoppers filling plastic bags with fruits from crates stacked in front of a small market.

Josh stopped and pointed at a cardboard box filled with spikey, pink balls the size of walnuts. "Wow, what are those?"

"Rambutan."

"It looks like a kind of jellyfish."

"It's a fruit."

"Is it good?"

"Yeah. Sort of like lychee."

"Lychee?"

"Think really juicy, really sweet cherries but white. We'll get some for dessert. Come on. We're almost there."

Nom Wah was already in full swing. The dining room was loud and busy, crammed with diners and waiters wheeling food carts trailing steam like skywriters.

"So dim sum's just like a buffet?" Jim asked.

"Sort of," I said. "A mobile buffet. The food comes to you."

"A lazy person's buffet," Dad said.

"Perfect," Winnie said. "I love dim sum already."

"How do you know what to take?" Josh asked peering into one of the carts as we followed the host to a large round table in the corner.

"Just take what I take," I said.

"Mommy likes the chicken feet," Zoe said.

"Phoenix claws," Mom said. "And don't knock them until you try them."

"Calling them something fancy doesn't change the fact that you're sucking on chicken toe jam." I snapped my chopsticks apart.

Jim pointed to one of the metal pots on the table. "Are these…"

"Tea." Mom poured a cup for Jim and one for herself, then handed the pot to Dad. "You should have seen Tris today. He was so great."

I took the napkin folded like a fortune cookie off my plate and ripped it open. "I didn't drop the knife on the floor. I don't think that qualifies as great." Did we have to talk about this?

Mom set her cup on the table, and tapped whatever she was really thinking in code on her lips.

Winnie eyed a cart piled high with bamboo steamers as it rolled by. "So how do you flag them down?"

"Like this." Zoe stood up and waved both arms like she was directing traffic on an aircraft carrier.

The waiter nodded and wheeled the cart to our table. "*Xiao long bao?*"

"Soup dumplings," Zoe translated.

"Do I want those?" Winnie asked.

Zoe nodded. "For her too," she said to the waiter.

"And me too please." Josh raised his hand like we were in school.

"I might as well try some too," Jim said.

Josh tipped his chair back against the wall and studied the room. "This place is so cool. How many carts do they have going at once? And do they all carry different stuff?"

"They usually have a few carts going around with the most popular stuff," I said.

Another cart stopped at the table. "*Char siu bao*. Pork buns?"

"Do we like those?" Josh asked.

"We do," I said.

I know. A meat baked good? But think about it: you eat meat and bread together in a sandwich all the time, right? This is just one step away from that, one step that will make you forget your *blah* roast beef on a roll forever, because shredded sweet-and-sour pork tucked inside a soft, doughy bun kicks that sandwich's butt.

Winnie pulled off the top of the bamboo steamer releasing a cloud. "*Ooh*, a meal and a facial all in one. Where's the soup?"

Zoe giggled.

Winnie spun around, her braid whipping around her neck. "What's so funny? The guy said, 'Soup dumplings,' didn't he?"

"Exactly." Jeanine bit off the tiny dough knot at the top of the dumpling. "Soup dumplings, not dumpling soup. The soup's *inside* the dumpling."

"I guess that's kind of a fun change, right, Winnie?" Jim said as he popped a dumpling in his mouth. He grabbed his water and guzzled.

"And *that's* why you bite the top off first," Jeanine said.

"Hot, but good." Jim nursed his tongue with an ice cube. "Almost worth losing that layer of skin from the roof of my mouth."

"I almost forgot." Josh dropped the legs of his chair to the floor. "Zoe was on TV with Brynn!"

"No way," I said.

"Yes way. Henry and I got to go in the bed." Zoe slurped soup from her dumpling.

"With her?"

"Uh-huh. *And* I told her a duck-duck joke, the one about the *quack* of dawn." She popped the drained dumpling into her mouth.

"But how? I mean, why did *you* get to go? It's not like you even watch her show."

Zoe rolled her eyes, then reached up and *boinged* one of her orange curls.

You can't blame Zoe for knowing she's cute. Wherever we go, people say so right in front of her like she's a puppy or something. And not just family and friends, strangers too. It's weird. It's even weirder when they try to touch her—I mean, usually just her hair, but still.

"*And* I told Brynn everyone should come to Petersville so it doesn't disappear."

"Go, Zoe," I said.

"It was awesome, and it was all on camera," Josh said. "Mom saw it on TV. She said Brynn even showed us with the signs and the Petersmobile."

"Get this," Jim said. "Cal called me after lunch to say traffic to the website went crazy after *Breakfast with Brynn*. So, put it here." He held up his hand for Zoe to high-five.

Zoe put down her scallion pancake and smacked Jim's palm.

"That's great. But that's just one day," Jeanine said. "If we want to create serious buzz, we have to be out there every day with the signs. *And* Tris has to keep winning, which is not going to happen if he goes out there and chokes again."

"Jeanine!" Mom said.

"What? He said the only reason he got through was because he didn't drop his knife. He was total krill."

Zoe spit the dumpling she'd just put in her mouth back into her steamer. "What's krill?"

"They're the little fish the shark eat. The girl with her own knives? Shark. The kid who choked?" Jeanine pointed her chopstick at me. "Krill."

"Jeanine, *sa soo fee*," Dad snapped.

"What? I was defining krill. How is that not helpful?"

"*You* know." Dad gave Jeanine the scary slow nod.

190

"But *I* don't." I had that shaken-soda feeling again. "I *was* krill."

"Tris," Mom said, but it sounded like, "Stop."

"What? I did. I choked. I trained and trained. Walter spent hours showing me what to do. And then when the time came, I couldn't do it. It's like textbook choking. So there! I said it!"

"Okay, we get it," Mom said. "Just maybe take it down a bit."

"Why?" My insides were getting fizzier every second.

Dad leaned in close. "Because you're yelling. In a restaurant."

"I am *not*!" I never yell. I go silent. I walk away. I disappear. I don't yell.

I looked around the table. Everyone was staring at me.

"I just meant," Dad said in his don't-scare-the-wildlife voice, "you're on the show for fun. You should have fun. Jeanine shouldn't take it so seriously."

"Where have you been? You think I've been training, getting up at five in the morning, because it's *fun*? I take it seriously, because it is serious!" I could hear myself now, how loud I was, but I couldn't turn myself down. "And the truth is: I did choke today. And what I need is not to do it again. What I don't need is for people to pretend I was great or that I deserve some kind of party!"

Before I knew it, I was on my feet, running through the restaurant to the bathroom and straight into a stall.

My whole body was vibrating. I had never yelled like that at my parents. Or anyone. Something inside me had broken, and everything had just rushed out.

I reached into the pocket of my jeans, pulled out a wrinkled square of paper, and unfolded it. Was this the closest I was ever going to get to the Donut Robot?

Even a little faded and torn, it still knocked me over. Ninety-six dozen doughnuts an hour! In my mind, I watched the hopper drop perfectly shaped doughnuts one after another into the oil, and the conveyor belt—

"Tris?" Josh's sneakers appeared under the stall door.

"Hey." This was embarrassing.

"You okay?"

"Uh-huh," I said, but I didn't open the door.

"You know, I get it. Why you… I get it." He didn't have to say more. Sometimes, *I get it* is all you need. Why did my parents not get that? My parents couldn't even admit there was an it to get.

I opened the bathroom door.

"I tasted a lychee," he said.

"Good, right?"

"Something about them kind of made me think of eyeballs, but once I got over that, yeah, I liked it."

Suddenly, I had an idea. "Hey, have you ever had a Cronut?"

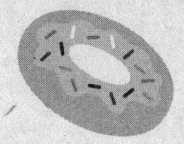
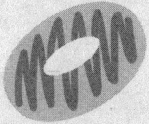

17

When the alarm on my phone beeped the next morning, I quickly turned it off and climbed down from my bed, trying not to rock the bunk too much.

"Josh," I whispered. "Get up."

He opened one eye. "What time is it?"

"I thought you wanted to get Cronuts?"

"You didn't answer my question."

"It's six."

He turned away from me and put the pillow over his head.

I ripped it away. "Come on. Get dressed."

Fifteen minutes later, we were zooming downtown on the 1 train.

Josh dropped into a seat, leaned his head back against the window, and closed his eyes. "Tell me again why I'm awake."

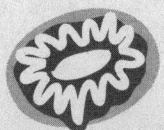

"Okay, picture a mind-blowing doughnut."

"Yeah."

"Now picture a mind-blowing croissant."

"Uh-huh."

"Okay, now imagine they had a baby. *That* is a Cronut."

Josh's eyes flew open. "Wait—are your parents going to freak if they wake up and we're not there?"

"I told Mom last night. I'm going to meet her and Dad at the fountain in front of The Food Connection just before nine."

"And what time does this place open?"

"Eight, but if you're not on line by seven, you'll never get one."

"And they only sell them in the morning?"

"Yeah, D.A. sells other pastries you can get whenever, but the Cronuts are really their thing. Oh, and cookie shots, but you can only get those in the afternoon."

"What's a cookie shot?"

"They bake these chocolate chip cookies in the shape of a cup and fill them with milk."

"That's awesome."

"Meh, it's fun. But it's kind of gimmicky. The Cronut is way better. You'll see."

Josh dozed for the rest of the ride to Soho. I made sure to stay awake so we wouldn't miss our stop.

The streets were still quiet when we came out of the subway station on Spring Street. During the day, Soho is packed, mostly with tourists, but the only people around now were some joggers and restaurants workers scrubbing tables at outdoor cafes.

As we walked to the bakery, I told Josh all about my first day on *Can You Cut It?*

"You should have seen these onions. They were the size of grapefruits. Okay, maybe not *that* big."

"Maybe Chef JJ wants to make sure nobody thinks she's favoring you, you know, because she knows your mom."

"Maybe," I said. "And then yesterday, with Mom, she was…"

"What?"

"I don't know. Like super…intense, but she's kind of always that way."

"Wait—is that for Cronuts?" Josh pointed to a line of people on the next block.

"Yup. Come on."

We jogged to the end of the line. It wasn't too long. Maybe about fifteen people. We'd definitely get our hands on Cronuts. I'd promised Mom we'd bring some back, but they limit you to two per person, so after Josh and I had eaten ours, that would leave two for the others to fight over.

We'd been waiting about five minutes when a short guy with a greasy ponytail stepped in front of us. "*Psst.* You guys looking for extra Cronuts?"

"Uh, yeah," Josh said.

The guy glanced quickly over his shoulder. "Twenty-five each."

"Dollars? For a doughnut?" Josh looked at me, wide-eyed. "Is that how much they cost?"

"No, thanks," I said to the guy. "We're good."

He shrugged and walked off.

"Wait, what just happened?" Josh said.

"He's a scalper."

"You mean like someone who sells tickets outside the stadium?"

"Yeah. He's got people waiting on line, and they'll buy doughnuts and then sell them to you for a mark-up, so you don't have to wait in line or so you can get more than two."

"How much do they cost in the store?"

"I think they're six-ish."

Josh turned around and watched the guy approach a family farther down the line. "Am I a bad person if I'm kind of impressed? I mean, something about it seems wrong, you know, like cheating, but still."

"Yeah, I get it. And it doesn't seem like such a big deal because he's not lying to anybody and, after all, we're only talking about Cronuts. But I'm pretty sure that people try the same scams with stuff like getting into schools or even getting new organs, and that's really messed up."

"You mean, like, *human* organs?"

"Yeah."

"There are human organ scalpers?"

"Jeanine was telling me about it."

"That's messed up."

"That's what I'm saying."

"Okay, no longer impressed with the Cronut scalper and considering calling the cops on him before he becomes a big-time scalper and moves up to hearts."

Josh and I bought our Cronuts and ate them on a bench.

"Okay, these are unreal." Josh licked sugar from the corners of his mouth.

"I told you. But this is definitely the best flavor I've ever had. They change it all the time. I didn't even know they made a Salted Dulce De Leche."

"It's just so..." He took another bite. "*Mmm*. Why don't *you* make Cronuts?"

"I would if I could. It's like, impossible to fry croissant dough.

You see all the layers, right? Well, if you fry them, they separate. Dominique Ansel came up with a way to do it so they wouldn't. He keeps it secret so nobody else can come out with a Cronut."

"Can we come here every day?"

My phone pinged, and I checked it.

It was a new email.

To: DoughnutBoy@TheDoughnutStop.com
From: WSiglinder@MajaniTea.com
Subject: Re: Urgent Investment Opportunity

Dear Mr. Levin,

   Thank you for your email. Unfortunately, at this time, Mr. Okello is not investing in any new ventures.

   Best of luck,
   Wally Siglinder
   Press Officer, Majani Tea

"It's not as if we expected it to work," Josh said, reading over my shoulder. "And it's not that he doesn't like our business, he's just not investing in any businesses other than his, I guess."

"Or maybe they just said that." I stood up. "We should go."

There was just one way for us to get the Donut Robot now: I had to figure out how to be a shark.

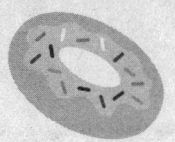

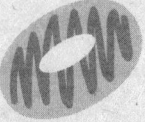

18

The Petersville Gazette

Vol. 1, Issue 19

SPECIAL EDITION: Reporting from the Petersmobile in NYC

Greetings from the Big Apple, where people can't get enough of the Petersmobile! It even caught the attention of the star of the morning show *Breakfast with Brynn*.

Team Petersmobile members Mayor Jim Partridge and General Store owner Winnie

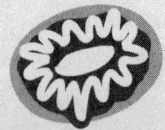

Hammond return to Petersville today. Join them Tuesday night at the Watch, Cut, and Quilt for a screening of video they took in NYC, including footage of *Breakfast with Brynn*'s tour of the Petersmobile.

Town Happenings

The Station House Special Pupusa Dinner: This Friday from 5:00–7:00 p.m.

The Doughnut Stop: Until further notice, Winnie Hammond will be operating the shop for reduced hours and selling only chocolate cream FYOs.

Gordy was gone. It was no surprise. We all knew he'd been eliminated, and it wasn't as if any of us really knew him anyway, but it still felt like somebody was missing. I don't think it was a coincidence that none of us sat in the chair he'd been sitting in the day before. I think we felt like it was his. Or at least I did. It might have been superstition with the others, like they were afraid Gordy's bad knife skills would rub off.

We weren't in the greenroom very long before Randy took us to the set to film Chef JJ announcing the next challenge, one they'd never done before, a Cloning Contest. We'd get a mystery sauce, and then we'd have twenty minutes to recreate it.

I'm pretty good at tasting different flavors, but I'd never tried to recreate a dish without a recipe. The good news was, since it was a brand-new challenge, we were all in the same boat.

Back in the greenroom for a break before the challenge, I started to wonder what sauce I'd make if I were trying to make it impossible for people to guess what was in it.

For starters, I'd use a ton of ingredients, harder to taste any individual one that way. Also, plenty of different spices.

What I needed to do was focus on ingredients and spices that were used together a lot in sauces. I didn't need to be able to taste everything. I just had to be able guess what spices were most commonly used with the ingredients I could taste. To prepare, I started running through spice combinations:

Clove, cassia bark, cumin, turmeric, and coriander.

Cayenne, oregano, thyme, and paprika.

"Guys?"

We all looked up. Randy stood at the door to the greenroom. "Chef JJ had to take a call so we're going to do an interview now. Keya?"

The second Keya and Randy were gone, Phoenix was on his feet, pacing and talking about how unfair Knife Skills Showdown had been. He was super worked up.

"So I think we should all sign this." He stopped pacing, pulled a piece of paper out of his backpack, and held it up.

"What is it?" Izzy asked. She was sitting on the floor reviewing flash cards with cooking terms like *dice* and *dredge*.

"It's a petition. It says we want Keya thrown off the show for using her own knives."

"This is isn't *Survivor*," Harper said. "We can't vote people off the island. Besides, it was in the paperwork. You're allowed to bring your own knives."

"But it never says anything about *specially-made* knives." Phoenix raised an *aha* finger.

"Here, I have something for you." Harper looked down, scanned the buttons on her jean jacket, selected one, and handed it to Phoenix.

"'Get over it'?" he read.

"You're welcome," Harper said as she rearranged her buttons to fill the space left by the one she'd given away.

"I think she's nice," Izzy said, not looking up from her cards.

"Who?" Harper said.

"Keya."

"Nice?" Phoenix said. "Do you get that she and her bionic knives are going to wipe the floor with you?"

"If you want to get rid of someone who has an unfair edge, why don't you vote him off the island?" Harper pointed at me. "Did you see Chef JJ and his mom together? Now *that's* unfair."

I didn't say anything. What could I say? It was true.

"Yeah, but she hates him," Phoenix said. "I mean, did you see his onions?"

"What if it's just an act?" Harper said. "Ever think of that? You know, to try to prove she doesn't favor him when she does?"

"If you think it's so unfair, how come you won't do anything about it?"

"Two reasons…" She counted them off on her fingers. "One: I'm not a whiner."

"*I'm* not a whiner." Phoenix jammed his hands in his pockets.

"Whatever you say," she said. "And two: he's never going to win."

"What are you, psychic?" I said. "You don't know who's going to win."

"You're right. But I can tell who won't win: the kid who was so nervous, he turned green before the first challenge. That's the kid who's going to choke."

"I'm not a choker."

"We'll see," she said.

Something burned at the back of my throat.

With Harper and Phoenix watching me, I walked out of the greenroom and headed for the men's bathroom at the end of the hall. There was a bathroom in the greenroom, but I wanted to be someplace I couldn't hear them talking about me.

I turned on the sink, slurped some water from my hands, then splashed cold water in my face.

The tip of my nose was sore, and it looked red in the mirror. Great. Just what I needed, a pimple right in the middle of my face.

I wet a paper towel and scrubbed at the spot. I don't know why. I knew I couldn't scrub it off. And I was just making it redder.

I gave up and went into a stall to use the bathroom. When I came out, Terrence was leaning against a sink looking at his phone.

"Hey," he said.

"Hey."

"How you feeling?" he asked, not looking up from the screen. "Second day can be rough because that first jolt of adrenaline's gone."

Static screeched out of the headset resting around his neck, and he yanked up the mouthpiece. "Hey! Didn't I tell you to watch it by that amp?" He pulled on the headset and listened. "No, no. Don't touch it. I'm coming right now..."

Terrence continued giving orders as he gave me a wave and walked out of the bathroom.

It wasn't until I started washing my hands that I saw the phone.

Terrence must have put it on the shelf above the sinks when he got the call on his walkie. I stood there for a second just looking at it.

Terrence was busy. Who knew how long before he noticed he didn't have his phone? And what if somebody had taken it by then? The right thing to do was to bring it to the set.

I dried my hands and picked up the phone. It sprung to life.

And it wasn't locked.

Before I knew it, I was reading the screen.

To: T.Glenn@CYCI.net
From: R.Merriman@CYCI.net
Re: Cloning Contest

T-

This mole sauce has a bunch of ingredients we don't normally stock. Please triple check that they're all there. List is copied below. If anything is missing and you-know-who blames me, I will personally carve CAN YOU CUT IT into your chest with a butter knife. 😊

-R

Black Mole Sauce Ingredients:
onions

garlic

guajillo chiles

mulato chiles

pasilla negro chiles

cloves

canela (Mexican cinnamon)

anise

allspice

plantain

prunes

bittersweet chocolate

almonds

sesame seeds

raisins

yerba santa leaf

I put the phone against my chest and looked around.

Click it off. Just press the button.

I tipped the phone forward just enough to see the screen.

Everybody knew there was chocolate in mole sauce. But yerba santa leaf? And who can taste three different kinds of—

Laughter, loud, close, and coming closer.

I jumped, dropped the phone, ran into a stall, and waited.

When more than a minute had gone by and I was still alone, I came back out.

The phone sat screen down on the tile.

I held my breath, squatted, picked up the phone, and turned it over.

No cracks. *Phew.*

I set the phone back on the metal shelf above the sink and rushed back to the greenroom.

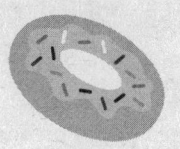
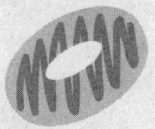

19

Interview with Tris Levin, Age 12, Petersville, New York:

Oh, no, I *do* feel good about winning the challenge. I just think maybe I ate too much chili or something. Do you think maybe we can do this later?

I ripped off my microphone and sprinted out of the room and down the hall, my eyes on the checkered tiles flying by. I didn't want to have to see anyone. At least Mom had texted that she and Dad would meet me back at the Petersmobile. I couldn't have handled them congratulating me in the parents' lounge in front of everyone.

My throat burned from the back of my mouth all the way down to my stomach.

What had I done?

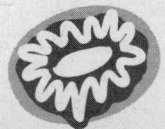

I spun around the corner and smashed into someone.

"Hey!"

I forced myself to look up. It was Dieter, his glasses lopsided.

"Oh, sorry."

"You are going to be killing someone this way. If you are going forward, you are looking forward, no?" He pulled the handkerchief from his blazer pocket and began wiping his glasses with it.

"I'm really sorry," I said, already backing away.

"Oh, good job today!" he called, stoking the fire in my gut.

"Thanks," I yelled over my shoulder.

I hadn't planned on... I couldn't even say the word for what I'd done in my own head, for what I was. If I tried hard enough I could almost convince myself I'd won fair and square.

And maybe I would have. There was no way of knowing now.

I would have recognized the sauce as a mole.

At least, I think I would have.

And for most of the challenge, I really believed I was only using ingredients I could taste. The thing is, I can't say that I wasn't looking for certain flavors because I *knew* they were in there. Maybe I tried to taste cloves because I'd seen them on the list. There was no way to know for sure.

It doesn't matter though because halfway through, I just gave up. Gave in?

Chef JJ came by my station. She was standing right behind me as I measured a teaspoon of salt over the saucepan. Then before I knew what happened, a blanket of salt covered the sauce.

"And *that* is why you don't measure ingredients over your pan," she said.

"*Tick-tock.*" Dieter tapped his kazoo on my clock.

I only had ten minutes left, and I was going to have to start from scratch.

I dumped the sauce, rinsed the pan, and ran back to the pantry. And this time when I went to grab the ingredients, I grabbed everything, not just what I'd tasted, but what I'd seen on that email, things I'd never have tasted, like the canela, the pasilla chiles, and the plantains. I never made a decision to cheat. I just did it and was moving so fast I didn't even have time to think about it.

And then it was over.

I'd managed to finish in time, and I'd identified more ingredients than anybody else.

I won. Izzy was out. And Phoenix hurled cooking utensils across the set like the Swedish Chef from *The Muppets*, or like the Swedish Chef's evil twin. I guess he thought the Cloning Contest was going to be his moment to shine. Skinny Jeans's on-camera tantrum was guaranteed to make a hit teaser for the show. Millions of people were going to get to watch Phoenix lose it over and over again. For sure, there'd be a GIF too.

Skinny Jeans was a know-it-all whiner. That wasn't on me. But I still felt bad, someone-holding-a-lit-match-to-my-tonsils bad.

I was at the elevators now. I pressed the button.

Cheater. It was all over the smudged face looking back at me from the elevator doors. How could anyone see me and not know? I tried out a few *I-won!* smiles, but they looked like someone was pulling strings on the sides of my mouth like some horror movie puppet. The rest of my face told the real story.

The elevator came, and I got on.

Then, just as the doors were closing, Keya rushed in, breathing hard, one of her Princess Leia rolls unraveling.

My stomach shot up into my chest as the elevator dropped.

"Congrats on your win! That was brilliant! I couldn't taste the chocolate in there under all those chilis."

Ping... Ping... Floors clicked by on the screen above the buttons.

"I've had mole before," I said to the cheater in the elevator doors.

There was a screech of metal grinding against metal, and the elevator bumped to a stop. The little black window flashed a neon-blue 22.

Keya's perma-smile disappeared. "Are we stuck?" She hit *L* again and again.

"Looks like it." I tried not to sound too happy. The truth was, I would have done anything to delay hearing everyone back at the Petersmobile tell me how proud they were.

Besides, it's not as if I hadn't been stuck in an elevator before, a tiny, rickety elevator it was easy to believe was seconds from plunging down the elevator shaft. Stuck in Grandma Esme's elevator had felt like a scene in a disaster movie. This elevator was shiny and spacious and sturdy and being stuck in it right then felt like a gift. Like the Earth had stopped turning and I was getting a time-out, but not the bad kind, the kind the Knicks get with two seconds left in a game they have no prayer of winning just so they can pretend a little longer that there's hope.

It was pretty obvious that, unlike me, Keya wasn't feeling all warm and fuzzy about being stuck in that elevator. She'd gone from hitting just *L* to pressing all the buttons and shouting, "Help!" The hand that wasn't madly punching buttons was gripping tight to the railing that ran around the elevator.

Keya was in the disaster movie.

"Can anybody hear me?"

"Here." I reached around her and pressed the one button she hadn't, the one marked EMERGENCY.

She gasped as if the button's purpose were to bring on the emergency, not deal with it.

A second later, we heard ringing coming out of the speaker below the panel.

She made a sound that was half exhale, half laugh.

"Hello, front desk, 611 Fifth Avenue," a man's voice said.

"Hey, we're stuck in one of the elevators," I said.

"Not again," he said. "Sorry, we had some maintenance work done recently and I don't know what they did, but ever since, we've been having problems. Just sit tight. We'll get you moving shortly."

"Okay, thanks." There was a click, followed by a long tone. I pressed the button again, and the noise stopped.

Keya took a deep breath and let it out slowly. "Sorry. I'm not much for elevators."

"Don't worry about it. This isn't my first rodeo."

"What's a rodeo?"

"Oh, sorry. I don't know why I said that anyway. It's dumb. My dad always says it. He thinks it's funny."

"Does that mean you're not going to tell me what a rodeo is?"

"Sorry." Why did I keep apologizing? "It's like a show. People ride bulls to see how long they can stay on before they get thrown off. It's like a cowboy thing. Cowboys are—"

"I know what cowboys are."

"Sorry." I slid down the wall of the elevator. We were going to be there a while. Might as well get comfortable.

Keya sat then too, not against one of the walls but cross-legged right in front of me, smack in the middle of the elevator, which no longer seemed so spacious. "Am I being thick? I still don't follow.

You've ridden a bull and this is useful to us in an elevator that has stopped working because…"

"Sorry." I cringed. Was that the fourth "sorry"? I'd lost count. "I'm being a nuddy. I just meant—"

"You're being a what?" Keya giggled.

My face went hot. Had I really just called myself a nuddy out in the real world? "Forget I said that. Please."

"I can't. I love it." Her smile was back at full wattage.

"You love what?"

"That word. *New*-Dee? Nuh-*Dee*?"

"You love 'nuddy'?"

"Yes!"

"You can't. You don't even know what it means."

"So what? I love the way it sounds. Nuddy. Nuddy. Nuddy. It makes my mouth want to smile."

She was always smiling anyway. How could she tell the difference? "Fine. I give up. You love 'nuddy.'"

"Does it mean something bad?" Her eyes got all big.

"No, it means 'idiot.' It's short for nudnik. It's Yiddish."

"Oh." Keya nodded like now it all made sense.

The panel's speaker made a clicking noise. Then the man came back on. "The repair guys are here, and they're working on it. Shouldn't take too long now."

"Okay. Thanks for the update," I called.

There was another click, then the tone. I crawled across the floor and pressed the button to make it stop.

"Can I ask you question?" Keya tucked a dangling bun behind her ear.

"Sure."

"What country speaks Yiddish?"

I burst out laughing.

"Oh, ha ha." She scowled at me. "There are twenty-two major languages in India. I bet you can't even name two!"

"No, no, you don't understand. I'm laughing because Yiddish, it's...it's not spoken anywhere, really. Not anymore. It's kind of a mishmash of German and Hebrew. I think it's only spoken now by like, really religious Jews."

"And your family's really religious?"

"No, my dad's not even Jewish. But through my mom we're... not really religious, but...connected. It's kind of hard to explain." I'd never even tried to before now. "We cook the foods, celebrate holidays—some at least—tell stories, and use some Yiddish words. If we worship anything, it's food."

"Oh, you're rememberers."

"Rememberers?"

"That's what you call people who use languages that aren't

really spoken anymore. That's my mom's thing. Languages, ones that are disappearing. We came here so she could teach at Yale University. Right now, she's working on a book. It's all about the last people on the planet to speak a particular language. They're called 'terminal speakers.'"

I couldn't help thinking about Petersville. Was there a word for the last people to live in a particular place?

Keya opened her bag, took out her phone, and began tapping away. *Click-click-click...*

Was I boring her?

"*Wir zenen stak,*" she read off the phone.

"What?"

"It's 'We're stuck,' in Yiddish. It's definitely not dead yet. It's on Google Translate." She held out the phone to me.

"Are you serious?" I looked at the screen. In the search box were the words: *we're stuck.* Then in the box marked Yiddish were Hebrew letters. "Wow. I didn't even know it was written in Hebrew."

"Look under the box. It tells you how to pronounce it."

I typed a sentence into the English box and hit Translate.

I did my best to read what popped up—*Aoyb ir gevinen, vos vet ir nutsn di freyz gelt far?*—and handed Keya back the phone.

She looked at the screen, then at me. "Plane tickets to England and India, so we can see family and friends whenever we want. You?"

"A Donut Robot."

"A what?"

"It's a machine that makes ninety-six dozen doughnuts an hour, so we, my friend Josh and I, can grow our doughnut business."

"Why doughnuts?" she asked. "That shop you started, The…"

"The Doughnut Stop."

"Right. I was just curious, what made you want to start a doughnut shop in the first place?"

Before I knew it, I was telling Keya the whole story, how my parents moved us to Petersville, how on the first morning in town I discovered Winnie's sign in the General Store advertising the chocolate cream doughnuts she didn't sell anymore, and how I finally got her recipe and then made it my own.

"I didn't want to move either," Keya said when I finally finished. "We moved to England from Hyderabad when I was eight. That was hard enough. Then, just when I was really settled, we moved to the States." She went quiet for a minute. "Do you come back to the city much?"

"A bit. But it's not the same."

"It's weird, right? Like even if you moved back, it would be someplace different. Every time I go back to Hyderabad, I keep trying to make it feel like it did before, but it just doesn't."

"I know what you mean," I said, remembering how I felt that

first night in the Airstream sleeping across the street from our old apartment.

"There *is* one place that still feels the same. My aunt's house in Leh. Up north. We only ever went for vacations, so going back for vacations now feels just like it did before. And I never spent time with anybody my age there, so it's not like when we go back to Hyderabad where I see kids who used to be friends but are really kind of strangers now."

Charlie popped into my head for the first time in months. Charlie, who had been my best friend since the Red Room in preschool. Charlie was a stranger now, a stranger who sent me invitations to birthday parties I knew he hoped I couldn't come to.

Keya and I were quiet for a while, and I noticed that the display screen wasn't flashing anymore. It was just black. Unsure whether this was a good sign or a bad one, I decided not to say anything about it.

Keya was tapping away on her phone again. "*Es iz nisht a tsufal,*" she read slowly, then handed me the phone.

In the English box were the words: *It wasn't an accident.* "What wasn't an accident?"

"I saw her, Chef JJ. She knocked the box of salt. She made you spill it."

"On purpose?" I'd been so focused on making the sauce and the clock, I hadn't even thought about how the spill had happened.

"Definitely on purpose," she said. "I know it didn't make a difference, I mean, you won anyway, but I just thought you should know."

She was right. It didn't matter, but not because I'd won. It didn't matter because I felt just as bad about cheating as I had before. Only now, I was confused too. I'd seen Chef JJ mess with contestants in all kinds of ways, but this? This was sabotage. Did she do this kind of thing regularly and they just didn't show it? Or was she just doing it to me?

"You know, everybody thinks Chef JJ favors me because she knows my mom."

"Yeah, she's definitely not favoring you. If anything, it kind of seems like the opposite. How does she know your mom again?"

"They worked together at a restaurant for a long time."

Just then, the speaker came to life with a low hum. "Hello?"

"Yup, still here," I said.

"We're good to go," the man said. "Just wanted to give you a heads-up."

"Great," I said at the same time Keya called, "Thank you!"

A moment later, the display began flashing again. Then the elevator shuddered into motion.

21...20...19...

We scrambled to our feet and faced forward like we were preparing to bow at the end of a play.

12…11…10…

"*New*dee?" the girl in the elevator doors said.

"Nuddy."

"Nuddy. Got it."

3…2…

The doors slid open. A man with worried eyebrows and Keya's face thrust his hand out to keep them from closing again. "Keya!"

"See you at the next rodeo," she whispered, then got out.

"You all right?" the man said as they headed for the lobby's side exit.

"I'm fine." I could hear an eye-roll, as if it had been some other girl in the disaster movie.

I started across the lobby in the opposite direction.

"Tris!"

"Yeah?"

Keya had stopped and was looking back. "People who work together for a long time don't always end up liking each other."

I stood there for a second, thinking.

"You understand what I'm saying?"

"Yeah," I said. "I think I do."

What Keya had said slowly sunk in as I walked across the plaza.

It wasn't until I got to the door of the Petersmobile that I remembered what was waiting for me on the other side, and the second I did, I felt every atom of my body pulling me the other way like the Airstream and I were the wrong sides of a magnet.

I forced myself to open the door.

"Your parents said you totally killed it." Josh gave me a high-five.

"I guess." I couldn't look him in the eye.

"Don't get too excited." Jeanine sat up in her bunk. "It's only the second challenge."

"Where is everybody?" I asked.

"At that diner on Fifty-Third. We're supposed to take you over there to celebrate. I'll be ready in a sec." Josh ducked into the bathroom.

"You know, the kids who waste their time celebrating they made it into the State Finals of the Solve-a-Thon never make it to Nationals," Jeanine said.

"I think Tris can celebrate a little," Josh called from the bathroom. "Besides, tomorrow is Fourth of July. He's off."

Jeanine sat at the table and began putting on her shoes.

"Hey, Jeanine?" I sat down next to her. "Did you ever hear Mom talk about why she and Walter left that place they used to work at with Chef JJ?"

"No, why?"

I told her what Keya had seen.

"She did *what*?" Jeanine was on her feet, one shoe on, the other still off. "We need to call someone! We need to file a complaint. Should we call the police?"

Josh opened the bathroom door. "What happened?"

I started to tell him, but Jeanine jumped in and finished for me. She was in hurricane mode.

"She can't do that!" Josh looked almost as whipped up as Jeanine.

"I think she can," I said.

"You know what we need to do." Jeanine was pacing now.

"What?" I said.

"We need to find out what really happened between Mom and Chef JJ."

"I think if Mom was going to tell us, she would have by now. I kind of get the feeling she might not even really know."

"And it's not as if you can ask Chef JJ," Josh said.

"We can figure this out," Jeanine said.

"Oh, really, how?" I said. "Go back in time? Not even you've cracked time travel yet."

Jeanine gave me a dirty look. "It's called research? Give me your phone."

"Why?"

"Just give it to me," she snapped.

I handed her the phone.

"What was the name of the restaurant Mom and Walter worked at with Chef JJ?" She tapped away at the screen.

"It was something Spanish. *El* something."

"Chef JJ Jordan restaurants," she said slowly as she typed. "Okay... The Parsonage, Wheat and Chaff, El Mariachi, Port—"

"*El Mariachi.* It was definitely El Mariachi."

"El Mariachi, 3 Columbus Circle," she read.

"Okay, so?"

Jeanine rolled her eyes. "Ever heard of field research?"

"Like when you collected animal poop and put it in the freezer?"

"It's called scat."

"I'll take that as a yes."

"Just think of it as a field trip," she said.

"To El Mariachi?" I asked.

"Exactly."

"Without the scat though, right?" Josh said.

"Without the scat," she said.

"Okay, then I'm in," he said.

"Me too." Whatever this was, I was pretty sure it was a horrible idea, but it was a horrible idea that would keep me from thinking about the horrible thing I'd done, and right then, that was all I needed to know.

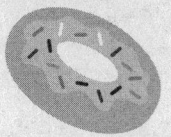
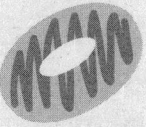

20

I had to hand it to Jeanine. The carousel was the perfect cover.

From the second we'd gotten to the city, Zoe had been begging to go to the merry-go-round, but it was a long walk through Central Park, and my parents were refusing to go until the weather broke. Since the night at Nom Wah, the city had been on a slow roast. Heat shimmered up from the sidewalk, and tar patches along the streets stuck to the bottom of your shoes. The weather was showing no signs of breaking, and neither were my parents.

If we offered to take Zoe to the carousel, my parents would be so happy they didn't have to schlep across the park themselves, they'd give us money for rides and ice cream and send us on our way, no questions asked. Or at least that was Jeanine's theory, and it sounded pretty solid to me.

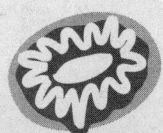

Our real mission? To find someone who worked at El Mariachi when Mom did, someone who might be able to give us a clue about how Chef JJ really felt about her.

Jeanine had checked the restaurant's website, and El Mariachi would be open for a special Fourth of July dinner that evening. So we'd go to the carousel—we'd have to or Zoe would pitch an epic fit—then head over to El Mariachi, which was only a short walk from there.

I barely slept the night before. I couldn't stop thinking about what I'd done. I'd gone twelve years without cheating. And now that I had, I worried it was like gambling or something—like now that I'd done it, it would be hard to stop.

Did cheating once make you a cheater forever?

When morning finally came, I couldn't get out of bed fast enough.

As Jeanine predicted, my parents flipped over our offer to take Zoe to the carousel. We'd all go to breakfast together at Barney's. Then we'd head to Central Park, and my parents would head to the Metropolitan Museum of Art to enjoy world-class art in world-class air-conditioning.

It wasn't until after breakfast when we were back in the Petersmobile grabbing water bottles that we hit a snag.

"Here." Mom handed me a tube of sunscreen.

"You just saw me put it on," I said.

"You're going to be out all day. You'll need to reapply."

"Fine." There was no way I was going to put more of this glop on, but I put it in the backpack I was using for water bottles and snacks anyway.

"And you should all wear hats," Dad said. "Seriously, this sun is no joke."

"Henry doesn't like hats. They hurt his ears." Zoe stood up from her bed, a sheet tied around her like a sling, a squirming lump hanging across her chest. "We're ready."

"Zo, you can't take Henry," Mom said.

"But he's never ridden the carousel."

"You're not going to be able to carry him around like that all day," Dad said.

"I can. Watch." Zoe marched from the back of the Airstream up to the driver's seat. "See!" She spun around, and Henry dropped to the floor.

"There's just no way, sweetie. I'm sorry." Mom tried to put sunscreen on Zoe's cheeks, but she pulled away.

"But I promised!" All the white spaces between Zoe's freckles were going red. This was headed nowhere good fast.

"It's okay," I said. "We can take him."

"See," Zoe said.

"How?" Mom asked.

I had no idea how.

Dad picked up Henry. "He's small, but there's no way Zoe can carry him around all day."

"What about my backpack?" I said.

"Do you think he'll be able to breathe in there?" Josh asked.

Mom inspected my backpack. "And if you keep it open, I think he'd get out,"

"No! I've got it." Jeanine popped up from the table. "Somebody give me a phone."

An hour later, we were walking single-file through Central Park along a narrow strip of shade, me followed by Jeanine, followed by her friend Kevin, followed by Henry riding in Kevin's sister's doll carriage, followed by Zoe, who was pushing the carriage, followed by Josh. The park was closed to cars because of the holiday, and the road was filled with bikers and Rollerbladers whizzing past.

We made a brief detour into a large playground at Seventy-Second Street to cool off in the sprinklers. Even Henry got a turn. The only one who didn't was Kevin, who refused to leave the carriage unguarded. According to him, kids had tried to make off with it in the past. It wasn't one of those doll strollers you see all around. It was a fancy, old-fashioned baby carriage that his parents had bought on a trip to London. I did notice it was attracting a lot of attention, though I couldn't tell whether that was because of the carriage itself or the bunny riding in it.

As we cut across the park toward the East Side, we could hear "Take Me Out to the Ball Game" floating across the baseball fields.

"That's it!" Zoe pushed the carriage faster, and the rest of us hurried to keep up.

"Boy, she's pretty excited, huh?" Josh said as we passed the popcorn cart by the carousel's ticket booth.

"You have no idea." I grabbed onto the back of Zoe's T-shirt to make sure I didn't lose her in the crowd waiting at the entrance. "Jeanine?"

"Over here." She poked her head between a man and a woman carrying identical girls in matching dresses.

Just then, the music stopped.

I tugged on the back of Zoe's shirt. "Hold on. We still have to get tickets."

"Here, give me the money," Josh said. "I'll get the tickets. You stay with Zoe."

I fished the cash my parents had given me out of my pocket and handed it to Josh.

"Wait, this too!" Zoe reached into the carriage, felt around under Henry and his blankets, and pulled out a ziplock bag filled with coins.

Zoe, it turned out, had been saving up for rides on the Central Park carousel ever since we'd moved out of the city.

So after Josh, Jeanine, Kevin, and I enjoyed the two rides my parents had paid for, Zoe stayed on for another eleven. Henry was done after three. I don't think Zoe minded though. Holding on to him cramped her style.

"Maybe she should stick to wooden horses," Josh said as Zoe flew past us for the zillionth time, calling, *"Yeehaw!"* and slapping her horse with the reins.

When she was finally out of tickets, we grabbed hot dogs at a stand by the ball fields and headed for El Mariachi.

Even though Zoe was pretty tired by then, she didn't complain that we weren't heading back yet because I'd promised that I'd get her Grom, the best gelato in NYC, on the way back to the Airstream if she was good and didn't ask questions. In case you don't know, "gelato" is fancy for extra-creamy ice cream. Kevin didn't ask questions because Jeanine had already filled him in.

El Mariachi was located on the thirtieth floor of a fancy

skyscraper that towered over Central Park. The lobby was lined with matching marble storefronts, and the air was deliciously cool. "Is this a mall?" Josh asked. "I didn't think they had malls in New York City."

"There are a few," I said. "Come on. I see the elevators."

"*Woah*," Josh said as we got off the elevator opposite a floor-to-ceiling glass wall overlooking the park.

"I think I can see Grandma Esme's building from here," Jeanine said.

"This would be a great place to watch the fireworks tonight," Kevin said.

"Let's get this over with." I pointed to the EL MARIACHI carved into a pair of dark wood doors.

A clear plastic garbage bag filled with folded white napkins sat just inside the restaurant's entrance. Chairs were stacked on tables. It was quiet, but somewhere a radio was playing. Glass lanterns hanging from pipes that crisscrossed the ceiling flashed bits of color everywhere.

"*Ooo.*" Zoe put out a hand and tried to close it over a piece of ruby-colored light.

"We're not open yet," a woman said. She was unloading wine bottles from a box onto the bar.

"Um, we're actually—"

"I'm looking for somebody who worked here with Kira Levin," I said over Jeanine. This might have been Jeanine's idea, but it was my mission.

The woman turned around, and seeing us for the first time, gave a little shudder. It was a pretty swanky place, and after a day in the park in one-hundred-degree heat, we were definitely too grimy for El Mariachi.

"Who are you looking for?"

"Someone who knew someone who used to work here, Kira Levin. She worked in the kitchen," I said.

"You're looking for someone who knew someone? That sounds kind of shady." She went back to unloading bottles.

Maybe it did sound a bit shady. In the movies, somebody looking for somebody who knew somebody was always bad news for one of the somebodies.

"It's for a project," Jeanine said.

"What kind of project?"

"We're doing this, um, special birthday project. For our mom," Jeanine said.

Jeanine really was a genius sometimes. Who wouldn't want to help kids complete their special project for their mom's birthday?

"I still don't get it," the woman said.

"We're collecting stories from people our mom worked with,"

I said, "or, you know, just knew at different times in her life, and we're gonna, um…"

"Make them into a book," Jeanine added.

"Right!" I said. "A book, album thing."

The woman stopped and wiped her hands on her apron. "What did you say her name was again?"

"Kira Levin," I said. "She worked here in the kitchen for a couple of years when it first opened."

"That's like, a *really* long time ago. Nobody in the front of the house is here from back then. Maybe somebody in the kitchen knew her. Some of those guys have been here forever. That long, I couldn't say, but you can go check." She waved a bottle in the direction of a swinging door at the end of the bar.

We all started for the kitchen.

"Hey, I can't let you all back there. Two of you. That's it. Tell them Kaitlyn sent you back." Then she ripped open another box and started unloading it.

"I'm definitely going," I said. "Who else is coming?"

"Jeanine should go," Josh said.

"Definitely," Kevin said.

"I don't think so," she said.

I couldn't believe what I was hearing. Jeanine wanted to take a back seat on her field research? "Then who?"

Jeanine reached out and *boinged* one of Zoe's curls.

Zoe growled and snapped her jaws at Jeanine's hand.

"And make sure people see her holding Henry. Trust me."

But Jeanine was wrong. The kitchen staff couldn't have cared less about Zoe and her adorableness. They didn't even look up when we came in.

Four men and one woman in white kitchen uniforms stood over shiny steel counters chopping and stirring to music on the radio.

"Excuse me," I said to a guy mincing a mountain of garlic cloves.

"Hey, hey, hey!" A man wearing a backward baseball cap barked from the oven where he was stirring an enormous pot. "What you talking to him for? He's got work to do."

"Um, Kaitlyn sent us back?"

The guy gave one more stir, covered the pot, and crossed the kitchen to us. His skin was so pale, it was almost see-through. "What do you want?"

"Sorry, I know how busy restaurants are before the dinner rush but we're…"

As I talked, the guy gave me the move-it-along sign with his finger.

"Hold up. Is that a rabbit?" he said.

Maybe Jeanine was on to something…

"Uh-huh." Zoe scooped up Henry and cradled him against her chest.

"I love rabbit," the chef said.

"Me too," Zoe smiled. "They're my favorite."

"Mine too." He put up his hand for a high-five.

Zoe smacked his palm, then stroked Henry. "Because they're so soft."

"And tender," he said. I could have sworn the guy was drooling.

"Anyway, I'm looking for anybody who might have worked here with my mom." We needed to get what we came for and get out of there before this chef started to rub Henry down with butter and rosemary.

"And who's your mom?" he asked.

"Kira Levin? She worked here with Walter Ramirez."

"Oh, the leeches." He laughed.

"The what?"

"You know what a leech is, right?"

"You mean those blobs that suck your blood?"

"Hey, everybody!" the chef yelled. "It's the little leeches."

The other cooks laughed.

The chef then went on to tell me about how Chef JJ had flipped out when Mom and Walter left El Mariachi to work at another restaurant, how she never forgave them, and how she still talked about "the leeches"—the slimy, bloodsucking blobs who betrayed her by going to work for the competition.

That's when I finally got it.

Chef JJ didn't let me on the show as some kind of favor to Mom. She'd let me on the show so she could torture me as payback for what Mom had done.

She was never going to let me win. I was going to lose, and she was going to make sure I suffered.

I'd never had a chance.

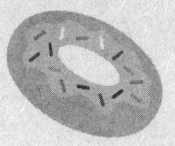
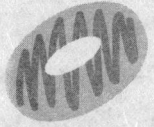

21

The Petersville Gazette

Vol. 1, Issue 22

SPECIAL EDITION: Reporting from the Petersmobile in NYC

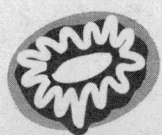

Featured Series

Things Most People Get Wrong and How YOU Can Get Them Right

By Jeanine Levin

You know how people are always saying it takes seven years to digest chewing gum? Wrong! Most gum isn't even digestible and it moves through your digestive tract at the same speed as anything else you eat. I'm not saying you should eat chewing gum. I'm just giving you the facts. Facts are freedom!

You're welcome!

Two more challenges. I just had to hold it together for two more challenges.

Why did I care anymore? Why did I even bother trying when I knew there was no way I could win? Because even if there was no chance we were getting a Donut Robot out of this, I could still reach millions of television viewers planning road trips. So until I got kicked off, I'd take whatever Chef JJ dished out and talk up Petersville every chance I got.

I'm not going to lie, I was mad—mad that I'd never stood a chance at winning, mad at all the hours of training that were for nothing, and mad at Chef JJ for holding on to some stupid grudge. I was even mad at Mom for being completely clueless.

But I also felt like this part of me that had been twisted up so tight it was hard to breathe had finally come loose. And it wasn't just because the pressure to win was gone. It was because the cheating was finally over. Nothing could erase the cheating. But the cheating would never end if I won. I'd see it every time I looked at the Donut Robot. It would go on forever. Now, at least it was over, because I was over. And that seemed fair.

Luckily, Josh and Jeanine were so worked up that they didn't even notice that I really wasn't, but even Jeanine knew there wasn't anything we could do about it. Nobody expected *Can You Cut It?* to be fair. It was like its own planet, and Chef JJ wasn't just the boss. She was the supreme ruler. It might not have been written in the contract we signed, but we all knew it.

Josh was already brainstorming our next move. How else could we get the money for the Donut Robot? How could we increase doughnut production without it? "Remember the Tea King," he told me. "There's always a way to make it work."

Listening to Josh, I wondered if I'd ever be able to tell him that I'd cheated. I didn't think I could make the words come out of my mouth even if I wanted to.

The day of the Egg-Off, we woke up to the sound of rain

thrumming on the roof of the Airstream. So when Mom and I left for the show, instead of heading out with their Petersville signs, everybody stayed inside, Dad and Jeanine working on the newspaper, Josh scribbling ideas to save The Doughnut Stop, and Zoe scrambling around the trailer building an obstacle course for Henry.

The Egg-Off rules were simple. Cook a perfect soft-boiled egg, with a set white and a runny yolk. There was no way to figure this one out. It's not as if you could watch the egg as it cooked inside its shell. You just had to know how long it took.

And, thanks to Mom's cooking lessons inspired by the hundred folds in a chef's hat, I did. One very long winter break, she'd taught me all one hundred ways to cook an egg. I'd gotten hooked on soft-boiled, something about dipping toast fingers into the creamy yolk kept warm inside the shell. I'd even started an eggcup collection. What's not to love about a breakfast food that has its own dish, particularly if that dish has feet and is wearing moose-head slippers?

A perfect soft-boiled egg takes five minutes—or three hundred "Mississippis" if you don't have a timer, which we didn't. The clocks were disabled for the Egg-Off.

Phoenix had never made a soft-boiled egg. Phoenix had never even eaten a soft-boiled egg. And from the nasty green film encasing his yolk, I'm pretty sure he'd never hard-boiled one either.

But instead of admitting he had no idea what he was doing, Phoenix doubled down, claiming he'd cooked his egg to oblivion in protest. His face turned purple as he ranted about how eating runny eggs could give you salmonella. It turned out his Swedish chef fit after the Cloning Contest was just a warm-up for his Perfect Egg-Off tantrum. Definitely GIF-able.

He was still shouting after Randy called, "Cut" and invited his parents to "remove their son" from the set and, ideally, the building.

That left Harper, Keya, and me.

The next day, Mom's alarm didn't go off, and we all overslept. Dad managed to get us from the Upper West Side to The Food Connection building without hitting a single red light, but even with me dressing on the way and skipping breakfast, I was still late.

"Thanks for joining!" Randy made a violent check on her clipboard, then pulled down the mouthpiece on her headset. "Okay. He's here."

Keya waved to me from her counter, and I waved back. There was no point in hating the competition anymore.

"Looks like somebody didn't get his beauty rest? Super juice?" Marco held out a clear plastic cup filled with a thick green... something. Whatever it was blurred the line between liquid and solid.

"No, thanks."

"You sure? Does wonders for the complexion. Even those circles." He waved the cup at my face.

"What circles?" Randy peered over her clipboard. "Oh, boy, you're not kidding. And what is that?" She pointed at my nose. Marco leaned in close.

My face went hot.

"Makeup!" Randy barked.

Without thinking, I leaned over the sink, turned on the water, and held my hands under the tap. I needed to do something, something that wasn't standing there watching Randy freak out because I had a pimple.

"What am I going to do? He looks awful," Randy said to Marco like I was deaf. "Should I cancel?"

"Don't worry. Barry will fix him up good as new. As long as it's not oozing. There's nothing he can do with crusty." Marco checked me out from different angles, clearly searching for signs of ooze.

I squirted soap on my hands again, then glanced quickly at Keya's station. At least she was pretending not to listen.

"It's a zit, not the plague," Harper said. Unlike Keya, she was clearly listening and had decided to weigh in. "It's a cooking show with kids. This can't be the first time somebody's had a zit."

Every time she said the word "zit," I felt like I was getting zapped with an electrical shock.

"You'd think," Randy said. "But I really can't remember this happening before."

"All those hormones, I guess," Marco said.

The word "hormones" was actually even worse than "zit," like two electrical shocks. *Zap. Zap.*

"Buddy, your hands are clean." Marco turned off the water and handed me a paper towel.

Clean, and numb.

"Makeup's here!" someone shouted.

Before I knew it, I'd been whisked off the set and into a chair in front of a lit mirror. I squinted against the light and watched as Barry, a mustachioed guy wearing a tool belt brimming with small brushes, examined my zit like it was a live bomb he had to disarm.

Randy gnawed a fingernail. "Is it crusty?"

"You *must* chill," Barry said. "It's not crusty."

I'm invisible. I'm invisible.

"*See*, it's fine." Marco massaged Randy's shoulders. "We'll just spray it with a little antiseptic. Barry will cake on some foundation, and we're good to go."

Just then, static exploded from Randy's walkie. "Go for Randy…" Her eyeballs bounced left and right as she listened. "No! No, no, no. We have a little…"

"Situation?" Marco offered.

"Situation," Randy repeated. "Okay. I'll tell you when to send them in."

My eyes were tearing from the light, so I closed them. Something cold squirted onto my nose and cheeks. Then I felt someone smearing it around.

"Okay, we're done here," Barry said.

I shaded my eyes and looked at myself in the mirror.

My face was the color of the inside of a cantaloupe, and there was so much gunk on it, you could scrape my name in it. "It's itchy."

"Tough," Barry said.

"No scratching. Up, let's go," Randy ordered, hustling me back to my station.

Harper took one look at me and burst out laughing. "You guys think he looks better now?"

I hate the competition.

The next minute, Chef JJ was marching across the set, Dieter a few steps behind. "Greetings, minions, seems like we were a little slow out of the gate this morning. Beginning to crack under the pressure, are we?" I guess that thought made her really happy, because she smiled a big, toothy smile right then. "You know what I always say…"

"If you're not standing the heat, get out of the kitchen," Dieter said.

Chef JJ rolled her eyes. "How many times do I have to tell you? It's *can't* stand the heat. If you *can't* stand the heat, get out of the kitchen!"

"If you *can't* stand the heat, get out of the kitchen," Dieter repeated.

"Well, I said it already now."

My face was so itchy, I swear I could feel the tickle in my teeth. I scratched at my palm and tried to convince myself it was my cheek.

Snap. The cameras began rolling.

"With only three contestants left, this is the last challenge before the East Coast regional finals. Whoever is sent home today will have come so far only to be sent home with nothing." One of the Transformer cameras stretched its neck toward Chef JJ as she crossed the set. "Let's see how Harper is handling the pressure."

"Bring it on," Harper said. "Oh, I have something for you." She unpinned a button from her jean jacket and held it up.

"'Winners never quit and quitters never win,'" Chef JJ read. "I like it."

Dieter took the button, wiped it down with a handkerchief, and handed it to Chef JJ.

"I knew you would," Harper said.

I liked it better when Harper was trash-talking. I'd take a trash-talker over a suck-up any day. It didn't even seem like Harper. Maybe the pressure was getting to her even if she couldn't admit it.

"And what about you, Keya?" Chef JJ said. "How are you managing?"

"A tad nervous." She smiled. "But I'm trying to just take each challenge as it comes."

"What a…nice attitude." The word "nice" made Chef JJ's mouth pucker like she'd sucked on a lemon. "And last, quite possibly least, Tris*tan*?"

"I'm just happy I'm still here representing Petersville, the best small to—"

"What's wrong with your face?" Chef JJ said, scowling at me.

"CUT!"

The next second, Randy was there, squeezing between me and Chef JJ.

"Tris was…pale this morning, so we had Barry give him a little extra."

"He is looking very"—Dieter's eyebrows inched down his forehead as he leaned in to study me—"apricot."

"Don't worry. We can even out the color digitally," Randy said.

"If you say so." Chef JJ was still examining my face like she was trying to identify something stuck to the bottom of her shoe.

When the cameras began rolling again, Chef JJ announced the challenge: One Ingredient Masterpiece. This was no surprise. One-Ingredient Masterpiece has been a challenge on every season except the first.

I'd found my one-ingredient masterpiece before I'd even gotten the email about the callback. I'd spotted it in one of Mom's *Sweet Life* magazines while clipping articles she'd marked. She'd promised me new hockey skates if I organized them in a binder for her. When I saw the recipe for a chocolate mousse made with just chocolate and water, I had to try it. Mostly because I didn't believe it would work. How could you make mousse without eggs or cream?

If I'm being totally honest, chocolate mousse *with* eggs and cream is better. But as long as the chocolate you're using is good, the one-ingredient mousse is too.

It was the perfect recipe for One Ingredient Masterpiece. The rules of the challenge allow you to use unlimited spices, herbs, oil, and butter to cook and flavor your one-ingredient, but I'd get extra points for a recipe that was truly a single ingredient. Water didn't count.

I couldn't wait to see the look on Chef JJ's face when I told her the mousse was just chocolate and water. It wasn't about winning anymore. It was about showing what I could do.

"Okay, folks, this is it. One Ingredient Masterpiece!" Chef JJ shouted. "Twenty minutes to transform one ingredient into something spectacular. Starting now!"

Dieter blew his kazoo. "Go and go and go!"

19:59…19:58…19:57…

We all ran to the pantry.

Chocolate…chocolate… I scanned the shelves. *Chocolate!*

I grabbed a semi-sweet bar and ran back to my station.

16:22…

I pulled a large mixing bowl from under the sink, filled it with ice cubes, then set a smaller glass bowl in the ice. Next I broke the bar into pieces and dropped them in a saucepan with one-third of a cup of water. Then I put the heat on low and stirred. I'd keep stirring until it was all melted. I wasn't taking a chance on burning the chocolate. There were lots of things you could fix, but there was no coming back from burnt chocolate.

Standing there stirring, watching the chocolate transform from solid to liquid right before my eyes, something happened. Everything else went away. It was just me and the smell of melting chocolate, lifting me up like a magic carpet.

11:37…

The chocolate was smooth now, so I poured it into the bowl sitting in the ice bath. Then I whisked it as fast as I could.

It's easy to whip too long. You have to catch it right when the surface goes shiny, which is usually about five minutes after you start whisking. If you miss that moment and keep going, the mousse turns grainy and thick, kind of like cement. Not bad tasting, just a little gritty, but tasty cement would never fly on *Can You Cut It?* so when I realized I'd let it go too long, I melted it again, and beat it until it was just right.

I finished right as the buzzer went off, and I felt myself smile, for real, no strings this time.

Chef JJ called Harper to the tasting table first.

"So what do we have here?" She peered over the plate Harper set on the counter between them.

"These are Szechuan dry-fried green beans." A bead of sweat escaped from Harper's hair and rolled down the side of her face.

Chef JJ sniffed the blackened beans, then raised an eyebrow.

"They've got a bit of a kick," Harper said.

Chef JJ speared a shriveled bean with her fork, put it in her mouth, and chewed.

And chewed…

Her eyes flew from the plate to Harper. Her fork clattered to the table. "Cracker!" she croaked.

Harper wrapped her arms around herself and hung onto her elbows.

Dieter pulled a sleeve of Saltines from under the counter, tore it open, and spilled a few into Chef JJ's hand. She mashed two crackers into her mouth at once, then held out her hand for more.

When she'd downed a quarter of the sleeve, she glared at Harper. "Have you *tried* these?"

Harper shook her head. "I didn't have time. Too much chili?"

"Here, you tell me." Chef JJ picked up a clean fork, speared three beans, then handed the fork to Dieter, who passed it over the table to Harper.

Harper took the fork and slid one bean into her mouth.

"Nice try," Chef JJ said.

Harper slipped the two remaining beans into her mouth.

We all watched as Harper chewed and swallowed, chewed and swallowed.

If Harper doesn't become a chef, she should become a professional poker player or a politician or anybody who has to bluff for a living. Maybe her throat was on fire, but you'd never know it from looking at her face.

"So what do *you* think?" Chef JJ said.

"I…I think." Harper reached for one of the glasses of water on the table.

Chef JJ elbowed Dieter. "Uh-oh, she needs a glass of water."

"I don't *need* one." Harper's voice was scratchy. "I would... like one."

"Oh, I see," Chef JJ said. "I misunderstood. I thought you *needed* water because eating these green beans is the culinary equivalent of swallowing a sword that has been doused in kerosene and lit aflame. *I* thought you'd created this dish as a form of torture for those who may have wronged you in a past life or killed a pet. But I see I was wrong. You don't *need* water, because this is exactly how you wanted your string beans to taste. Is that right?"

Harper nodded slowly. You had to hand it to her. She was so going down—we all knew it—but she would not let Chef JJ break her. She wasn't going to blubber like Izzy or lose her cool like Phoenix.

But Chef JJ was done with admiring Harper's toughness and cooking technique. People watched the show to see her crack kids, and it was time to crack Harper.

Chef JJ tapped her fork against the plate. "So this is exactly the way you like them, is it?"

"It is," Harper said, standing so straight, it seemed like she'd actually grown a few inches.

"Okay, so finish them." Chef JJ pushed the plate across the table. "Now. Eat every last one."

"What is this, an eating challenge?"

"Sure."

"You know what I'm thinking?" Dieter turned to speak directly into the camera. "Harper is"—he waved his arms like he was conducting everyone watching this at home on their couches—"making excuses."

"I don't do excuses." Harper picked up the fork and began gobbling string beans.

In seconds, streams of sweat were rolling down her face. "Fine! Fine!" She waved the fork in the air. "I misjudged the chili. Happy now?"

"Yes." Chef JJ sighed, then smiled. "I am."

"CUT!"

When we came back from break, it was my turn. I brought up the mousse in two small bowls and set them on the tasting table.

Chef JJ sniffed, dipped her spoon into the mousse, then held it up to the light, and inspected it. If it were at all grainy, she definitely would have seen. I couldn't see any sandy spots, and if she did, she didn't say so.

Finally, she put the spoon in her mouth, then swallowed, and gave a little shrug. "Meh."

"Meh?" I said.

"You know, 'meh' as in, 'ish.' Not good, not bad. Just kind of there."

"But I only used one ingredient. Just the chocolate."

"That's true. But that's really its *only* virtue, isn't it?" This wasn't an act. She really wasn't impressed. "Although after those green beans, I guess you get points for not causing me physical pain, so there's that. Bravo for blandness."

Dieter clapped. "Bravo for blandness!"

Yay, me. I moped back to my station.

"Keya, let's see what you've got back there."

Keya walked forward slowly as if she had a book balanced on her head, and when she passed, I realized why. On her tray were two mugs filled to the brim with a steaming, foamy liquid.

I couldn't believe it. Keya was fancying things up with those milk frothers? For a while, each new restaurant in New York Mom dragged us to was serving everything bubbly—soups, sauces, anything that could be frothed, was. And it did look cool, but you know what bubbles taste like? That's right, nothing. No way Chef JJ was going to fall for an airy, tasteless soup, no matter how cool it looked.

Chef JJ put her face over the mug and inhaled. "Cardamom?"

Keya nodded.

"And turmeric?"

Keya nodded again.

"And…" Chef JJ took a long sniff. "Cloves?"

"Just a bit."

"I'm intrigued. Tell me what we have here."

"It's a spiced butter tea. My own take on traditional butter tea that we drink in the north of India. I spend summers there with my aunt. I don't love the classic version. It's more…practical, keeps you hydrated, warm. Gives you energy. This one does that as well, but it tastes quite nice too. At least, I think it does."

"Let's see." Chef JJ picked up a mug with both hands and sipped once…twice…three times. "Taste it," she said to Dieter.

He picked up the second mug and drank. "*Mmm*. Ginger too, yes?"

"The tiniest pinch," Keya said.

"And brown sugar, right?" Chef JJ sniffed again at the steam rising from the cup. "Salt too. I love the sweet and the spice. It's the perfect blend."

Keya lit up like someone had flipped a switch. "Really? You don't understand. I did so much experimenting before I came up with the right mix of everything. My family is so sick of tasting it for me."

I wanted to taste spiced butter tea. It sounded so different from anything I'd ever had. And it was Keya's own creation. If I didn't get to taste it now, I never would.

Chef JJ took another big swig. "I'm having this every morning for breakfast."

Keya giggled.

"I'm serious. You're writing down the recipe. This is my new go-to breakfast." Chef JJ took another gulp. "Congratulations! You're the winner of One Ingredient Masterpiece!"

"Really!" Keya jumped up and down, and before Dieter could stop her, she threw both arms around Chef JJ, who froze like she was playing Red Light, Green Light.

"CUT!"

"Remember? No touching!" Randy shouted as she raced out from behind the lights.

"Oh, sorry!" Keya quickly let go. "I just—"

Chef JJ put up the stop hand, then hurried off the set, muttering to herself.

"I'm really sorry," Keya said to Randy. "I just forgot. Is she going to be okay?"

"Sure, she just needs a nice, long decontamination."

"She has a special machine," Marco explained. "Kind of like a—"

"TMI, Marco," Randy snapped.

"Sorry." Marco pretended to zip his lips.

"We were done for today anyway," Randy said. "Keya, Tris, go get some rest. The finals aren't until Friday so you have tomorrow off. Harper, you need to stick around for your interview."

"The finals? You mean, I'm in," I said.

"Wasn't that obvious?" Randy said. "Bravo for blandness, remember?"

"It was obvious to me," Harper said. "I knew I was out the moment she compared eating my green beans to swallowing flaming swords."

Harper was out, and I was in the finals?

What was I thinking? My cheating wasn't over. I was still there on the show. I was there, and Izzy, Phoenix, and Harper were gone. Who knows who'd be in the finals if I hadn't cheated?

"Good luck." Keya was holding her hand out for me to shake. "May the best chef win."

My hand felt like it was weighted down with bricks, but I forced myself to lift it and give her hand one quick shake. "Oh, yeah, good luck to you too."

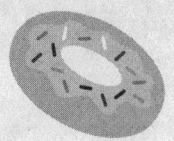

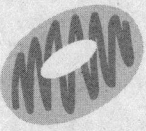

22

Mom would not stop talking.

She started the second I saw her in the greenroom and was still at it when we sat down for dinner at Barney Greengrass. Dad had taken Jeanine, Josh, and Zoe to a movie so it was just the two of us.

Did you see JJ's face when she ate that string bean?

Wouldn't you love to taste that tea? I'm dying to try it.

Do you think JJ will hire a bodyguard to protect against future hugging? Keya's not getting within two feet of her again.

Not sure Mom even noticed that she was both asking and answering her questions.

Zippo came out of the kitchen tying an apron around his waist. "Hey, *so* how's my favorite TV celebrity?"

"He's in the finals!" Mom said way too loud. Was "bravo for

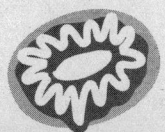

blandness" really something the entire Upper West Side needed to celebrate?

"Way to go." Zippo gave me a thumbs-up. "The usual?"

I nodded. It didn't matter. I wasn't hungry. Plus, I was worried what would come out when I opened my mouth. I had that fizzy feeling I'd had that night at Nom Wah.

"You know what? I'll have matzoh ball soup tonight too," Mom said. "And a side of white fish. And an onion bagel."

"Coming up." Zippo noted the order, put the pen back behind his ear, and disappeared into the kitchen.

"I'm so excited for you," Mom said.

And I could tell she really was, and it killed me, sitting there with her looking all proud and happy and clueless.

We'd all agreed not to tell Mom what we'd learned at El Mariachi. She would have felt awful, and it wouldn't have changed anything. But I still couldn't help blaming her for how everything had gone down. I'm not saying it was her fault that I cheated. That was all on me. But who knows what would have happened if I hadn't gotten on the show because Mom was Chef JJ's leech? Wouldn't everything have been different?

Mom took out her phone, dialed, then held it to her ear.

"Hey, Walter, just checking in." As she listened, the hand that wasn't on the phone went to her mouth. "Okay, so I guess we just need to pull back to four mains. And cut the steak… I'll think about it." *Tap. Tap-Tap.* "We may not have a choice… Yup, the finals! I'll tell him." She looked at me and pumped a fist in the air. "All right. See you then." She swiped the screen and put the phone on the table. "Walter says hello and congrats."

"What else did he say?" Was she really going to have that conversation right in front of me and then pretend everything was great?

Tap-Tap. "Just some restaurant stuff."

"Like what?" I swear I could feel my molecules zooming around faster and faster, bashing against my insides, looking for a way out.

"Don't worry about it."

"Are you cutting the menu again?"

"Business is…" *Tap. Tap.* "We're just experimenting. You know how I am."

"Right, this is all just about how you are. Because everything is great, right?" In my lap, I squeezed my napkin into a tighter and tighter ball.

Tap-tap-tappity tap. Mom studied me. "What's wrong?"

"Nothing's wrong. Everything's great, right?"

Zippo appeared and set the soups on the table. Each bowl held one enormous matzoh ball surrounded by a narrow moat of chicken broth.

I blew on a spoonful, sipped it, then waited for the Barney's chicken broth to make the world go all happy endings, at least for a bit.

And I waited and waited…

We had the next day off, and by the time I woke up, light was pouring into the Airstream. I rolled over.

Josh jumped up from the table. "I have an idea. It's not the Donut Robot. But it's something."

I swiped crud from the corners of my eyes. "What?"

"Sorry. I've been up for a while. Cronut?" He picked up a paper bag from the table and shook it.

"You got Cronuts?"

"I woke up early."

I climbed down from the bunk. "Where is everybody?"

"They went to your grandmother's. Something about your cousins coming into town today? They said they'd call later about where to meet them."

That was the last thing I needed: a family reunion where all anyone would want to talk to me about was *Can You Cut It?*

When I came out of the bathroom, Josh had put the Cronuts on a paper towel on the table.

"You didn't eat yours yet?"

"I'm not going to lie. It took superhuman strength to wait—oh, I almost forgot." He pulled a carton of milk from a plastic bag on the floor and set it on the table.

"It's okay. I only drink milk with chocolate."

"It's not to drink. It's my idea for The Doughnut Stop."

"Milk?"

"Not just any milk. Mohawk River." He tapped the container.

"Still not following."

"Okay. So, all day yesterday, I was reading about the Tea King and Majani, trying to get ideas and coming up with nothing. Then last night, we came back from the movie, and I was lying in bed googling on my phone, and there was this video of Okello giving a speech, and it was all about how Majani was Krakow, and about how if he'd started the business someplace else, it would be a completely different business. He said he used Krakow's strengths, the people there who needed Majani to succeed as much as he did. And that's what made me think of Mohawk River."

"You lost me again."

"Okay, so Mohawk River is a dairy collective up by us. It was created by the dairy farmers in upstate New York because they couldn't compete with the big dairy companies by themselves, so they work together. And that's when it came to me. What if we created our own sort of collective to make the doughnuts? What if The Doughnut Stop was like Mohawk River and we could find people to make the doughnuts for us?"

"You mean, other people would make *our* doughnuts in *their* houses and then we would sell them?"

"Yes! We'd be able to give people jobs *and* grow the business."

"But how are people going to know how to make the doughnuts?"

"Easy. You'll teach them."

Now that I understood the plan, I began to run through it step-by-step. "So, first we'd have to find people who are good at following directions. I mean, they don't even need to know how to cook. They just have to be able to follow really specific directions. Then we train them and get them the ingredients they'll need. We'll probably have to buy some equipment for them too."

"We can get a wholesale discount and probably buy the equipment secondhand." Josh grabbed a pad and pen from his bed and began to take notes.

"Then they just show up to deliver the doughnuts wherever we need them. We could even take advantage of different people's home locations. Remember how Betsy's in Crellin said they would sell doughnuts if we ever had enough? Maybe we could find someone who lives close to Crellin to make doughnuts for her."

"Yes!" Josh scribbled away.

"You know what? I think this might actually work."

We spent the next couple of hours hammering out a plan. We even wrote a want ad to put in *The Petersville Gazette*:

NEEDED: PART-TIME WORKERS

Want to be a part of The Doughnut Stop team?

Flexible hours. You can work from home. No experience necessary.

Interested? Send email to DoughnutBoy@ TheDoughnutStop.com.

At noon, we headed to Barney's for latkes and eggs and onions, then climbed an enormous rock in Central Park, and sat there making to-do lists.

We were just starting to come up with a budget when my phone buzzed with a text.

Dad: So dinner is at G-Mare's at 6. Wear something nice, okay? Or at least clean-ish.

I'd gone almost a whole day without thinking about *Can You*

Cut It? and I didn't want it to end. I didn't want to have to sit there while my aunts and uncles and cousins and grandmother grilled me about what it was like on the show and told me over and over how awesome I was for making it to the finals.

Me: I don't think we're coming
Dad: Come
Me: Dad I really don't feel like it
Dad: Everyone wants to see you
Me: Sorry
Dad: Not okay. Command performance. We won't stay late
Me: I really can't

A second later, he was calling. Even though I really didn't want to, I picked up. "Dad, Josh and I are—"

"I understand this is not how you want to spend the evening. *Tant pis.*"

The French was out. A bad sign.

"It's more than that," I said.

"You know what, Tris, you're not a little kid anymore. Sometimes you just do stuff because you have to."

Unreal.

"Tris?"

If he thought I had to stop acting like a little kid, why was he always trying to sell me fairy tales about everything being all rainbows and unicorns?

"Can you hear me?" he said.

"Fine, see you there," I said, and hung up.

The dinner was just as painful as I'd thought it was going to be. Everyone wanted details about the callback and each challenge. And they all told me how "great" it was that I'd made it to the finals. *Can You Cut It?* was basically the only thing anybody wanted to talk about. Plus, my grandmother was doing the traditional French meal with like, a zillion courses, including separate ones for salad, cheese, and dessert, so we were trapped at the table forever.

I didn't say a word to Dad at dinner, or on the way home, or back at the Airstream. He went right on talking to me though, either not noticing I wasn't talking back, or pretending not to.

That night, I dreamed I was back in Petersville on Main Street right under the traffic light. Dr. C was there too, hammering away at a huge block of something that looked like yellow soap. I was just standing there, watching bits of the stuff fly off as Dr. C carved away at it. Then he stepped back, turned to me, and said, "It stinks, doesn't it?"

That's when I saw: *it* was me. Not all of me, just my face, as big as a refrigerator, carved out of a giant hunk of butter.

"Tris?"

I could even smell the butter.

"Tris, wake up."

I opened my eyes. Hanging above me was a white paper bag. Someone shook it, then pulled it away.

There was Dad, Muppet-smiling down at me. "Went all the way to Patisserie Claude. Got there just as these babies were coming out of the oven." He put his face in the bag and inhaled. "Still hot."

I looked around. Everyone else was still sleeping. "What time is it?"

"Early. Come on. Get dressed," he whispered.

I rolled away from him. "I don't have to be there until nine." I was awake enough now to know I was still mad.

Dad shook the bag again. "When was the last time you had a real croissant?"

I didn't say anything.

"Come on. I want to show you something."

"Is this another command performance?" I said, face to the wall.

"Just come."

Clearly, that was a yes. I was too awake to go back to sleep anyway. And it *had* been forever since I'd eaten a real-deal croissant.

Dad had driven us to The Food Connection building as we slept that morning, and he waited outside by the fountain while I got dressed.

Last day, I said to myself in the bathroom mirror as I pulled on my PETERSVILLE, THE PLACE TO EAT T-shirt.

By the time I got outside, the *Breakfast with Brynn* crowd was already lined up along the sidewalk. Since the heat wave had broken, there were even more Brynn-heads, and instead of trying to snake my way through them, I took the long way around to the fountain.

"Here." Dad handed me a croissant wrapped in a paper napkin.

I sat down beside him on the bench that circled the fountain. Water shot high into the air behind us, spraying the back of my neck with a cool mist.

I pulled the croissant apart slowly, watching the greasy layers stretch, break, and rebound. You can't do that with those tasteless, horn-shaped rolls people pass off as croissants. The trick is butter, sheet after sheet of butter, and Claude never skimps.

I dropped a piece onto my tongue. It melted like a snowflake.

Dad popped the last bite of croissant into his mouth, stood up, and brushed flakes off his pants. A good croissant will leave you covered in golden flakes.

"What's that for?" I pointed to a cardboard tube tucked under his arm.

He took a deep breath, pulled a paper scroll from the tube, and unrolled it flat on the bench.

It was a photo of a box, an enormous, bright orange box sitting on some grass with two matching lawn chairs beside it. Judging from the chairs, the box was about the size of the Airstream. "What is it?"

"Guess?" Dad waggled his eyebrows.

"Do I have to?"

"Come on. It's more fun this way."

"I guess it sort of reminds me of those things on boats they use to ship stuff."

"*Ding! Ding! Ding!*" Dad was in full-on game show host mode. "Exactly! Shipping containers. Okay, hold that thought." He rolled up the photograph, unrolled another scroll, and held it flat. "Now, what do you see?"

Jeez, how many rounds of this game were there? "A room? A bed. A chair. A desk."

"Yes? All in the"—he held up the first scroll—"shipping container."

"Still not getting it. Why are people hanging out in shipping containers?" This had sycamore syrup all over it. Where was Jeanine when I needed her?

"Because it's cool and cheap and environmentally friendly!" Huge smile.

"And orange."

"You can get them in any color." Even bigger smile.

"And claustrophobic."

"You can put in as many windows as you want. You can even make one whole wall glass."

"You want us to live in a shipping container?"

"No. It's Petersville's first inn!" He opened a third scroll, a map of town. "See, these..." He tapped four rectangles labeled *A*, *B*, *C*, and *D* in the field beside The Station House parking lot. "...are cottages."

Whatever this was, Dad must have been working on it for months.

"So here's what I was thinking. No matter how incredible we make the Petersville experience, no matter how much publicity we get, Petersville is too far for most people to travel to just for the day. If we want visitors, we need to provide a place to stay." He jabbed at the rectangles. "And a place to eat." He pointed to The Station House.

"You're opening a motel where people stay in shipping containers?"

"It's not a motel. It's an inn. But, yes, I am! Remember Barton?"

"Who?"

"My friend from college?"

I didn't, but I nodded anyway because I didn't see how it mattered either way except that if I said that I didn't, I'd have to listen to some story about who Barton was and the good old college days.

"Well, Barton is starting this company that refurbishes shipping containers, and he's going to give the first four to us at a huge discount because he needs to drum up business. They'll come and take lots of photos to put on his website!"

"How long have you been planning this?"

"I don't know. I guess I first got the idea the night of the meeting."

"And you've been keeping this secret all this time?" It didn't make any sense. This was actually a good idea, and way more useful than the paper. Why did he wait so long to tell anybody about it?

"I didn't want to tell you until I had everything finalized, until I knew it was going to work out."

Now I got it. He didn't tell me until he could say it was going to be great.

"Why does it matter when I told you?"

I stood up. I couldn't look at his smiling face one more second.

How could he not get it? I didn't need another story from him about how everything was great. I didn't need a story about how he figured it all out. Those stories were never going to help me. What I needed was a story about how he messed up so bad, he had no idea how to make it right or even which direction he had to go to get to right.

"What's wrong?"

"Nothing. I…" I couldn't tell him what was wrong. He didn't want to know. He wanted me to believe his stories about rainbows and unicorns. He wanted me to say school was a ten; he wanted me to write articles for his paper; he wanted me to believe that I could win a Solve-a-Thon if I tried. "I gotta go. I can't be late."

He looked at his watch. "You won't be. You still have time."

I backed away. "Yeah, but I need…I need some time, you know, just by myself before, to focus."

"Oh, okay. That sounds smart." He started rolling up his plans. "We can talk more about this later."

"Sure. I'll catch up with you guys at the parents' lounge after," I said, still moving away.

"Hey, Tris, hold on a sec." He came closer. "Are you sure you're okay? You look—"

"Yeah, sure. I'm…great."

Then I turned and walked away.

I heard him call something after me but I didn't stop. I think it was "good luck."

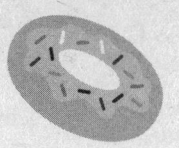

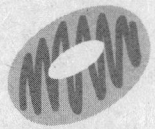

23

Zooming up in the elevator, I tried to shut Dad, all sycamore-syrup smiley, out of my head.

As much as I wanted to run out of The Food Connection building right then and forget about *Can You Cut It?* forever, there was something I needed more.

I needed to prove I deserved to be in the finals. I needed to prove that I'd deserved to be there all along.

It wouldn't erase what I'd done, or make it okay, but maybe it would help me figure out how to face up to it.

Just outside the greenroom, my phone buzzed with a text from Josh: "Concentrate! Create! Crush the Competition! Concentrate! Create! Crush the Competition!"

Me: Jeanine?

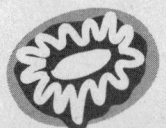

Jeanine: I borrowed Josh's phone

Me: What happened to believe and achieve

Jeanine: Time to step it up

Me: She's never going to let me win. U know that right?

Jeanine: U don't need her to say it to know if u won.
B THE SHARK.

My throat went tight. Jeanine had been cheering from the beginning for all kinds of reasons, for Petersville, for herself for coming up with the idea in the first place, but this time felt like it wasn't for anything but me.

Me: Thanks

Jeanine: Never, never give up 😊

Jeanine was right. I could do more than just prove I deserved to be there. I could blow Keya out of the water. I could win, even if Chef JJ was never going to say the words. I just needed to focus.

Be the shark. Be the shark.

I threw open the door to the greenroom.

"*Gut margn!*" Keya was sitting in the armchair closest to the door smiling her freakishly friendly smile. "That's 'good morning' in Yiddish."

Did she really expect that we'd come in here before the finals and talk like we had when we were stuck in that elevator? Everything was different. We were winner and loser now, even if we didn't know who was who yet.

I headed for the couch on the other side of the room, as far from Keya as I could get. Sharks were loners.

"My mother says there's some great Yiddish plays people still perform. Maybe you already know that, but I thought I'd say, just in case you didn't." As Keya chattered on, she wandered over to the food spread, which was down to one lonely plate of lemon poppy mini muffins. "I'm knackered. I couldn't sleep at all last night. Can you believe this is it?"

I stayed quiet. Sharks were not chatty.

"Tris?"

I reached into my pocket, pulled out my headphones, plugged them into my phone, and turned up the music as loud as it would go. Then I closed my eyes.

A few seconds later, I felt the earbuds being ripped out.

"What's your problem?" Keya's freakishly friendly smile was gone. Finally.

"What's *my* problem?"

"Just because it's down to the two of us, you won't even talk to me?"

"Don't you get it?" Why did I have to explain this to her? "We're winner and loser. That's it. The person who crushes and the person who gets crushed."

"That's…that's the most…" Her face had gone all splotchy red. "You know what? You *are* a newdy!"

"A nuddy!"

"Whatever!" She threw my earbuds at me, then marched over to the table, grabbed a bottle of water, and guzzled it down.

I jammed the earbuds back in my ears.

Not sure whether I felt like a shark, but thanks to me, I was pretty sure Keya did now.

Keya and I went straight to our stations when we got to the set.

"Anybody else feel the temperature drop when these two walked into the room?" Marco said. "Tension and loathing. I like it." He rubbed his hands together.

"*Brrr.*" The medic, April, pretended to shiver, then flashed Marco a grin that was more gum than teeth.

"Hey, Keya, Tris," Terrence called from offset. "I didn't have time to come by the greenroom. Come give me your phones."

"I got it," Marco said and came around to collect our phones.

As I washed my hands, Chef JJ and Dieter walked onto the

set. Randy hurried out from behind the lights and showed them something on her clipboard.

Just then, I remembered that my parents were in the room, Keya's too, probably. The finalists' families were invited onto the set for the last challenge.

I squinted into the lights but couldn't make out anything past the Transformer cameras.

"So." Marco knocked his fist into my shoulder. "You ready?"

"I'm ready," I said louder than I'd meant to in a voice that didn't even sound like mine. Maybe it was the shark's.

"I got to say I never thought you'd make it this far. I mean, remember Knife Skills Showdown? Yowza. That was not pretty."

"Thanks," I said as if Marco hadn't just told me he'd been betting against me from day one.

Marco was never going to see me as a shark. Just like Harper had said, we'd all been chosen to play a role, and that's not the one I'd been chosen for. Harper was the shark. I was the choker, and Marco wanted to make sure I didn't forget it. Maybe it was just trash talk, but it didn't matter. It had worked.

I felt that burning at the back of my throat.

Randy clapped her clipboard over her head. "Okay, everybody! This is it."

Snap!

The cameras began to roll. The sound guys dangled their mics over our heads.

Chef JJ was talking but I could barely hear her. My heart was beating too fast and too loud. I could feel it all over my body, in my ears and in my hands.

I love competing. I am a shark. I am a shark…

Who was I kidding? I could say that stuff a million times. It wouldn't make it true.

And then from far away, I heard something that changed everything: "…Killer Cupcake Competition!"

The burning in my throat disappeared.

My heartbeat jumped back into my heart where it belonged.

Whatever I'd been feeling, just the word *cupcake* had cured it.

I didn't need to compete to make cupcakes. I didn't need to hate anybody to make cupcakes. I didn't need to be a shark to make cupcakes. I'd been making cupcakes before I could spell "cupcakes." I had cupcakes running in my veins.

There was no question. I'd make the peekaboo cupcakes I'd invented for Henry's birthday. Zoe had begged me to make an FYO cupcake like the FYO doughnuts, so I'd created a cake with buttermilk that had enough "give" you could fill it with cream without the whole thing falling apart. I knew the recipe by heart because I'd spent days perfecting it.

One problem: Chef JJ wouldn't get the same kick Zoe did from filling the cupcakes. She'd probably even accuse me of leaving them unfinished. Easy fix: I'd just fill them myself, use a special tip, and swirl cream like soft serve ice cream around the top to hide the hole. That would even look good. Plus, you wouldn't know about the cream on the inside so there'd be extra *wow* when you bit into it.

But which flavor cream? Butterscotch was too risky. Even though Chef JJ didn't taste the butterscotch cream at the callback, I was pretty sure she'd remember it, and I didn't want her to think I was a one-trick pony.

Chocolate? Not after I'd made the mousse.

Then it came to me. Mocha! Chef JJ was always sending people to get her coffee. No way she wasn't a mocha fan.

Mocha peekaboo cupcakes. Killer.

I ran to the pantry and got everything I needed for the cake: eggs, butter, sugar, buttermilk, vanilla, flour, baking powder, and salt. I'd make the cream while the cupcakes were baking.

I whizzed through making the batter and didn't look up even once to see what Keya was doing. In no time, I was sliding the cupcake tin into the oven.

50:28...50:27...

I ran back to the pantry and searched the shelves for instant decaf coffee. That's what I used to give The Doughnut Stop's chocolate cream a little kick. I figured for mocha cream, I'd just increase the coffee.

Where was it? My eyes raced along the shelves a second time.

No instant coffee at all, but there was ground coffee so I grabbed that and everything else I needed for the cream, including shredded coconut that I saw and suddenly knew would add the perfect flavor and crunch, toasted and sprinkled on top.

I ran back to my station, praying there was a coffee maker there that I'd just missed. I'd never actually used a coffee maker, but I'd watched my parents make coffee every day of my life. It wasn't rocket science. I could figure it out.

After a thorough and completely useless search of the cabinet, I flipped the HELP sign over the back of the sink like Randy had told us to do.

A few minutes later, Chef JJ and Dieter were standing at my station. "My best guess?" Chef JJ said to Dieter. "Tristan here is wasting valuable time with whatever this is."

"*Tick-tock*," Dieter sang.

"I need a coffee maker."

"'Need' is a funny word," Chef JJ said.

"See, I'm ma—"

"Forget it. Make something else," she said and walked off.

What was I thinking? Of course she wasn't going to help. I could have said I didn't have any spoons and she would have told me to cup my hands and start stirring.

46:02…46:01…

Forget Chef JJ and whatever fancy coffee machine she was holding hostage. I didn't need either. I was making coffee, not building a rocket launcher. Making coffee without a coffee machine wasn't impossible. I didn't *need* a coffee maker. People made coffee for centuries before coffee makers, right?

Just like the Tea King said, my solution didn't need to be pretty or fancy. I just had to make it work.

I could do that. The only must-haves were water and ground coffee and…

I ran to the pantry. No filters.

But what are filters? Just paper, right? I could totally Swiss-Family-Robinson filters.

I ran back to my station, filled a pot with water, and put it on a burner on high. While I waited for the water to boil, I tore off a ribbon of paper towels and folded them into a large square. I twisted the square into a cone and tried to picture myself filling it with coffee.

I couldn't be holding the cone when I poured in the boiling water. It would rip. And, worse, I'd burn myself. I needed to be able to sit the cone in something that would let the water flow through. I needed...

I was just about to look in the cabinet again when I noticed the sieve I'd used to sift the dry ingredients on the counter.

Yes!

Okay, what next? Something to catch the coffee as it dripped. I went through my equipment again. Mixing bowls. Measuring spoons. Measuring cups. A measuring cup!

I rinsed off the sieve, lined it with the paper towel cone, and spooned five tablespoons of coffee into it. I needed it strong. Then I sat the sieve on top of the measuring cup and slowly, very slowly, poured the boiling water over the coffee, stopping every few seconds to let the liquid drain into the measuring cup.

While the coffee dripped into the cup, I toasted the coconut in a pan over low heat, stirring every few seconds so it didn't burn.

Bing!

I turned off the burner, moved the coconut to a cool spot, and opened the oven.

Out floated a warm, vanilla-y mist. *Mmm.*

I slid the rack out and studied the cupcakes. They looked perfect, all puffed up with just a hint of gold around the tops. A toothpick slid into the center of one came out clean. Done!

42:14...42:13...

I popped the cupcakes out and left them on a wire rack to cool while I made the cream.

At first, the chocolate drowned out the coffee flavor, so I kept adding coffee and tasting until it was the right balance. On the fifth try, I hit mocha. It was good, rich and sweet, but there was no *wow*. Something was missing.

"Hello?"

I blinked. Dieter was waving his hand in front of my face as I sat there with a spoon in my mouth staring into space. *"Tick-tock."*

"I'm thinking."

"Don't hurt yourself." Chef JJ sneered.

She could say what she wanted. I was in my own world, someplace where I was supreme ruler and her words were just noise.

What was that secret ingredient that would take this mocha cream to the next level? Vanilla? Boring. Cinnamon? Maybe. Almond extract? Wrong. Nutmeg?

I ran back to the pantry and grabbed a small knob of fresh nutmeg.

Dieter whistled as I grated it. "Fancy."

Chef JJ zapped him with one of her looks.

I knew I was on the right track just from the smell.

I wasn't sure how much I'd need so I added it to the cream in pinches, mixing after each one and tasting.

One: no change.

Two: there but only a ghost.

Three: *shazam*!

The chocolate and coffee were still the strongest flavors but now there was also this peppery spark.

I'd found a plastic case marked "Cake Decorating Supplies" in my equipment drawer. Inside was a pastry bag, a plastic sleeve with a big opening on one end and a small one on the other, and a bunch of metal tips with different shaped holes. I chose a tip with a sunburst hole, screwed it into the small end of the bag, and spooned the cream into the big end. The sunburst would give me the perfect wavy ribbon of cream to wind around the top of the cupcake.

Now came the fun part: I pushed the tip into the center of the top of the cupcake and slowly squeezed the bag, emptying cream into the cake until the top began to rise. Then I lifted the tip out and spiraled frosting out from the hole until I'd covered the top, then I spiraled back in again.

I felt my mouth spreading into a bigger and bigger smile.

Suddenly, I got that feeling you get when you know you're supposed to be doing something but aren't and can't even remember what that thing was.

I looked around.

20:02...20:01...

Time! I'd completely forgotten about the clock. And the competition.

And I didn't care.

For the first time in so long, everything felt right. Like I knew who I was and what I was supposed to be doing, and as long as I kept doing it, everything else would be okay.

I made the last circle of icing over the spiral tower, set the cupcake down on a clean white plate, and sprinkled it with the toasted coconut.

Perfect.

Eighteen minutes left, and all I had to do was fill and ice one other cupcake.

For the first time since the challenge began, I checked what Keya was doing.

She must have just taken her cupcakes out of the oven because she was still wearing oven mitts, but she wasn't taking the cakes out to cool, and I could see why. They were shriveled down in their little cups and though their edges were brown, their centers looked wet and foamy.

She had time to make another batch if she hustled. But she wasn't hustling. She was chewing on her bottom lip, staring down at her shrunken cupcakes. Maybe she was trying to figure out what had gone wrong—it didn't made sense to start again until she knew what had happened.

Come on, Keya. Come on. Go through the steps in your head. Find the mistake and get moving.

I don't know if she couldn't figure out what went wrong, or if she wasn't even trying but two whole minutes later, she was still just standing there.

Before I knew it, I'd put down the pastry bag and was headed over to Keya's station.

"Hey, you can't do that," Marco said behind me. His voice sounded different, like for once he was saying something he hadn't practiced in front of a mirror.

At the front of the set, Chef JJ and Dieter were offering tips on making buttercream frosting and didn't seem to notice that the Transformer usually trained on my station was swinging sharply to the left.

April the medic saw me though, and beat me to Keya. "Go back to your station," she said, blocking me. They were definitely going to have to edit this out.

"Keya?" I said over April's shoulder.

She didn't say anything. She was still staring at her sad cupcakes.

"Look—"

April poked me in the chest. "I said, 'Back to your station.'"

I backed up as if I'd given in, but then circled around the front of the counter to Keya's other side. "You have time to make another batch."

"Why do you care? You want to crush me, remember?" She shoved the tray across the counter. "Now, you have."

"We just need to figure out what went wrong."

"Dude, you won," April said. "Let it go."

"C'mon, before you-know-who has a fit," Marco whisper-yelled. He was standing behind April, his arms crossed, hands squeezing his bulging biceps.

"April, Marco, you're in the frame. Back up," said the camera guy shooting from the far end of the counter.

"Were they just yellow cupcakes?" I reached into the cabinet and pulled out some clean mixing bowls.

"What are you doing?" Keya said.

I couldn't explain even if I wanted to so I just started scooping flour into one of the bowls.

"I'm not fooling around," Marco warned. "Get back to your station now."

"It's over," Keya said.

It wasn't over. It couldn't be over, not until Keya had some cupcakes for Chef JJ to taste so she could declare Keya the winner.

"Okay, what's next?" I looked around the counter. "Baking powder! There's no baking powder. That's what you forgot."

Right then, someone jerked my shoulders from behind. I stumbled back, trying to catch myself, but couldn't get my feet under me.

The next thing I knew, I was on the floor, looking up at Marco, who looked as surprised as I felt.

"I'm so sorry," he said. "I didn't mean to…" He reached out to help me up, but before I could take his hand, someone was swatting it away.

"What's wrong with you?" It was my mother, right there on the set, standing over me, glaring at Marco like she was going to rip his head off.

"Mom?" I felt my face go hot. "You're not… What are you—"

"Are you okay?"

"I'm fine." I got up off the floor.

Mom looked me up and down. "You're sure? Because sometimes it takes a while when—"

"I'm *sure*."

Mom put her hand on her heart and took a deep breath, then spun around to face Marco, her eyes flashing from worried-mom back to monster-mom. "Don't you ever—"

"*What* is going on here?" came an icy voice. "And dear God, what are *those*?" Chef JJ pointed to Keya's cupcakes.

My mother, Marco, and April all started talking at once.

"Enough!" Chef JJ snapped. "Randy!"

"Right here." Randy was standing behind the camera chewing a pen cap to shreds.

"Get the leech back to her seat."

"Who?" Randy said.

"I meant…" Chef JJ had a look on her face I'd never seen, and before I could even say what it was, it was gone. "Get Kira, Tristan's mother, back to her seat."

"I'm sorry, did you just call me a leech?" Mom said to Chef JJ.

"Kira, do you know how much it costs if we don't finish filming on schedule? Are you going to pay for that?"

"She did call you a leech," I said. I wasn't going to cover for Chef JJ. "That's what she calls you and Walter."

"Why?" Mom looked more confused than upset.

Chef JJ's nostrils flared. "Why? Why?" she taunted. "Because that's what we call people who suck your blood and then move on without so much as a thank-you."

For a few moments, Mom didn't say anything, and neither did anybody else.

What happened next was pretty much the last thing I think anyone expected: Mom burst out laughing.

"What's so funny?" Chef JJ snapped.

Mom gripped her side like she had a cramp and kept on laughing. Tears streamed down her cheeks.

"What is so funny?" Chef JJ repeated, a vein across her forehead pulsing.

"*Ooo. Ooo…*" Mom gasped for air. "Walter and I open a bottle of champagne every April 12 to celebrate the day we quit! He's going to love it when I tell him you call *us* 'the leeches.'"

"Stop it! Stop laughing!" That vein in Chef JJ's forehead looked like it might burst.

"Mrs. Levin, um," Randy said, "maybe you could, you know, go back to your seat so we can finish filming."

Mom wiped her eyes. "Oh, right. Yes, of course."

As Randy led my mother, still chuckling, off the set, Samara brought Chef JJ a glass of water.

"Let's just get this over with." Chef JJ pushed the glass away, splashing Samara. "Tristan, get back to your station so we can declare"—she shivered—"declare you the winner."

This wasn't how it was supposed to go down.

"Come on. Go, get." Chef JJ shooed me away.

"But—"

"Just get back over to your station so we can finish!" She gave me one zap with her ice-blue lasers, then spun around, and stomped to the tasting table.

Randy began barking orders at everyone.

"People," Terrence called, "we're going to reset the clocks and cut to where Tris left his station."

I still hadn't moved.

"What did you make?" Keya asked.

"Cupcakes filled with mocha cream."

"Save me one?" She gave a small smile.

And right then, I knew what I had to do.

"Hold on." I went back to my station, got the finished cupcake, and brought it to Keya. "Congratulations," I said as I handed it to her.

Then I walked off the set.

"Where is he going?" I heard Marco say.

"Tris!" Randy called. "We don't have time for a break now."

"Get back here!" Chef JJ yelled.

I stopped at the door, but I didn't turn around. I didn't think I could do it if I had to see their faces.

"I cheated!" I called over my shoulder.

Now it was really over.

The second the door closed behind me, I realized I had no idea what came next. Get to the elevator. That was all I had.

Had the cameras been rolling when I walked out? Did they have me on film saying I cheated?

I looked down. Jeez. The mic was still clipped to my shirt. I ripped it off and dropped it onto a desk as I rushed past.

If they'd gotten me on film, would they show it on TV? Would I have to explain to everyone, not just in Petersville, but every person I ever met for the rest of my life what I'd done?

Would I hear, "Hey, aren't you the kid who…" everywhere I went forever?

What had I done? Why didn't I just make crappy cupcakes? Why did I always have to make everything so hard?

I jumped onto an elevator just as the doors were closing.

Now what?

Bing… Bing… Bing.

The elevator doors opened, and I ran. Across the lobby. Through the revolving door. And out into the plaza.

Then I stopped. I had nowhere to go.

The Airstream was right out front with Josh, Jeanine, and Zoe waiting for me inside, but I couldn't face them. Not yet.

I walked to the fountain, sat on the bench, and hunched over so

I couldn't see anything but my shoes.

So what happened? That's the question I was going to get again and again, not just from Josh and Jeanine and Zoe but Zippo, all my aunts and uncles and cousins, my grandmothers, Winnie, Jim, and everyone in town.

I couldn't imagine getting the words out even once. How would I be able to say them over and over? Maybe I could wear a sign, like one of those big poster boards they use to advertise stuff in Times Square. Or maybe I could email everyone, and beg them to never, ever ask me about it in person because I might drop dead from humiliation right in front of them.

"Hey."

I didn't look up but I could see Mom's red sandals and Dad's Nikes.

I waited for them to say something else, to ask me what I'd done, to tell me I had to go back and apologize to everyone, to tell me how disappointed they were.

I'm pretty sure time moves extra slow when you're waiting for something painful like that—like when you're waiting to get a shot at the doctor—but I really did feel like I was sitting there for hours waiting for them to say something.

After a while, they sat down on either side of me, and I finally looked up.

"Chef JJ is a nightmare. Always was, always will be," Mom

said. "I guess I just thought, I don't know, time passes. You forget. People change. It feels like a million years ago."

"Not to her, I think," I said.

"No kidding," Dad said.

Just then, over Dad's shoulder, I spotted Keya and her father crossing the plaza, and in a flash, I was up and running.

"Keya!"

She turned, then saw me and kept going.

"I'm sorry," I said to her back as she walked away. "Can I just tell you what happened?"

Her father stopped, so Keya did too.

"We have to go," she said.

I could tell by the look on her father's face that they didn't, but I couldn't blame her for wanting to get away from me as fast as possible. "I just wanted you to know how sorry I was. Really, really sorry."

"Okay," she said not looking at me. "But we really need to go. Bye." Then she walked off, pulling her father along with her.

"Bye," I said.

I walked slowly back to the bench and sat down between my parents.

"You okay?" Dad said.

The question threw me. "I don't know."

"Say more," Mom said.

Couldn't they just punish me or yell at me? "Can we do this later?"

"No," Mom said. "We can't."

"Fine. I feel like I won't ever be able to fix this," I said to my shoes.

"Didn't you just fix it?" she said. "If you didn't deserve to win, you shouldn't have, and you made sure you didn't. What else is there to do?"

"But I still feel so…" There was no word for how bad I felt.

"I bet," Dad said. "Did I ever tell you about that time I shoplifted?"

My head snapped up. "No."

"I was seven. G-mare said she wasn't going to buy me any more comics. She thought they were dumb, and they just piled up around the house. And I was obsessed with this superhero series, Secret Wars. Anyway, there was a new one out, and I just had to have it. It seems silly now, but then, I don't know. I was at the newsstand, and I just took it."

"Did you get caught?"

"More like I cracked. Uncle Philippe saw me with it and asked how I got it. I think I was actually dying to get it off my chest. He made me take it back and apologize to the owner. Thirty years later, I still remember exactly what that felt like."

"Did Uncle Philippe tell G-mare?"

"Nope."

"Yeah, see, that was just you and Uncle Philippe and the guy who owned the newsstand. You apologized, and you moved on. G-mare, Uncle Philippe, the whole world is going to know what I did, and I will never get past it."

"It will blow over in no time. You'll see. It's gonna to be fine." Dad waved me off like I'd spilled something, like it was nothing a roll of paper towels couldn't make disappear.

Something inside me that had been ripping little by little tore wide open. "No, it's not gonna be fine!" I shouted. "It's not fine if they show me on television saying I cheated, if the whole world finds out that I'm a liar. That's not fine! The Doughnut Stop is not fine! Mom's restaurant is not fine! Petersville is not fine! So just stop saying it is."

"Tris, I told you—" Mom started.

"I *know* what you said. But I can see things aren't fine, and I don't want to waste time pretending they are. That doesn't help."

Dad pinched his chin and gave me a long, hard look. "Okay."

"Okay?" I felt like I'd been running hard at a wall bracing for impact, and the wall had just moved, and now I was falling.

"What do you want to know?" he asked.

"Everything," I said. "And start from the beginning."

And they did. And it wasn't anything I didn't already know, but that was never the point.

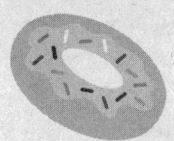

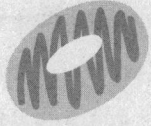

24

The Petersville Gazette

Vol. 1, Issue 52

Town Happenings

Celebrate the opening of The Petersville Inn (the town's very first!) with doughnuts, Saturday at 2:00 p.m.! Party at The Station House with tours of the cottages running every thirty minutes.

Harry Potter Marathon at the Watch, Cut, and Quilt this weekend. Watch all eight Harry Potter movies while you get the "Harry," "Ron," "Hermione," or "Bellatrix" haircut, then make a quilted portrait of your favorite character.

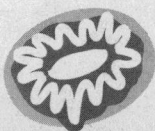

Things Most People Get Wrong and How YOU Can Get Them Right

By Jeanine Levin

This will probably come as a shock to many of you so you may want to sit down. Ready?

The Earth is not perfectly round. Never was. Never will be.

It's kind of squashed at the poles and swollen around the equator.

I know. It blew me away too.

You're welcome!

Join The Doughnut Stop Team!

Wanted: drivers to deliver doughnuts to Albany three mornings per week. Interested? Send email to DoughnutBoy@TheDoughnutStop.com.

The morning after the *Can You Cut It?* East Coast finals aired, I jerked awake.

It was here, the day I'd been dreading since I'd walked off the set.

My room was still dark, and the house was quiet, but I got

out of bed and pulled on some clothes. There was no going back to sleep. I'd head into town and get to work early. The sooner I started this day, the sooner I'd have it behind me.

Going back to school would be rough too, but at least kids had a whole month to forget what they'd seen on TV.

Who was I kidding? What they'd seen wouldn't have been forgotten. The best I could hope for was that it had faded a bit.

By the time I made it outside, the birds were up, and an orange glow was beginning to ooze over the mountains.

I grabbed my bike from the shed and walked it across the grass to the dirt road that zigzags through the woods down the mountainside. I don't care how good a BMX-er you are. Riding a bike down Terror Mountain is not an option.

Even though the sun was barely up, the air was already thick and wet. By the second zag, my hands were slick on the handlebars, and I stopped to wipe them on my shorts.

At least there were no clouds. Nobody would show up for Dad's big opening if it rained.

As I rode to town, my brain replayed clips from the night before.

In case you didn't catch it, the answer to your question is, yes, everything that happened at the Killer Cupcake Competition was captured on film. Everything.

And, yes, it did all end up in the final episode, on television screens all over America, probably all over the world, possibly even the universe. This very second, an alien family on Mars could be chuckling as they watch Mom karate chop Marco away from me, a move I somehow missed in the moment.

And, no, the *Can You Cut It?* folks weren't mad about what happened, actually the opposite. They loved it. A producer I'd never met called us the day after we got home to tell us so. "Just like *real* reality," the guy said. He was especially into that part where I walked off the set, because it was obvious that nobody had planned it or knew what to do next.

The reason he was calling? Not to warn us that they had the whole Killer Cupcake Craziness on camera and would be airing it. Oh, no. He was calling to inform my parents and me that we were in violation of our contract, and that I needed to return to film my "exit interview." Oh, and if I didn't, Mr. Real Reality explained, The Food Connection Company would sue my parents. At first, I thought this was a joke. Then I saw Dad's face.

So Dad took me back to the city to film my exit interview. It was with Randy and Mr. Real Reality. What they wanted to know most of all? How I'd cheated. I think they were hoping for something like I got dressed up as a ninja, scaled the outside of The Food Connection building in the middle of the night with toilet plungers attached to my hands and knees, picked the lock on the roof door, and then hacked a computer.

They looked pretty disappointed when I explained how the recipe had just popped up on Terrence's phone in the bathroom. "That's *it*?" Randy said.

"That's it," I said. She looked so sad, I couldn't help but add, "Sorry." Randy wasn't that bad.

As I biked up the hill just outside of town, one clip flashed through my brain, something else I'd missed seeing that day, Keya's face at the moment I admitted I'd cheated. It was like a punch in the stomach.

What did she think now? She must have watched the show, seen the interview.

Phoenix had probably already called The Food Connection offices to demand that they give him another shot because I'd cheated, though he'd bombed the Egg-Off all on his own. The person who most deserved another shot was Izzy since she was the one eliminated in the Cloning Contest, and I said so during my interview.

And Harper, what did she think? I shivered imagining her staring me down on her television screen as I admitted what I'd done.

The lights in The Station House were on when I rode up. It had to be Walter. Mom never got up this early to come to the restaurant, and both my parents' cars were there when I left home.

I leaned my bike against the porch and went inside.

"It's me!" I called, ducking under the counter.

Walter was at the stove, stirring something.

"No pupusas?"

"*Atol de elote.*"

The sweet, milky corn drink wouldn't fill me up like pupusa, but it was a close second to my favorite of Walter's dishes from back home.

Walter brought two mugs down from a shelf and poured the steaming liquid into them. He spilled a bit on the counter and wiped it up with the dishrag draped over his shoulder.

"Careful." He handed me a mug.

I blew into it. The color reminded me of Keya and her butter tea and how I'd never get to taste it.

When it had cooled a bit, we both drank.

"Stop!" Walter slapped his hand over the mug like he'd just realized the drink was poisoned.

"What is it?"

"Not enough cinnamon," he said like this was a matter of life and death.

After a couple of cranks of the cinnamon grinder over each cup, he handed mine back.

"Okay now?" I said.

Walter took a sip. He tick-tocked his head, then smacked his lips. "Not bad. The corn is perfect though. Riley picked it yesterday."

I drank some.

"Better?"

"Mmm."

"It's good to see you smiling this morning. How are you holding up?"

"I'll live."

It was the only time Walter asked me anything about the show, even though given the amount of time he'd spent training me, he of all people had earned the right to ask whatever he wanted to know.

"Hey, what are you doing here?" I said. "Isn't the restaurant closed today for Dad's opening party?"

"Oh, I…" Walter looked around the kitchen like he was trying to locate something he'd misplaced. "I'm making a surprise for the, uh, party."

"Oh, yeah. What?" Walter was a lousy liar.

He cracked a grin, then snapped the dish towel at me. "You got me. You know, my mother always said *atol de elote* was so sweet, it could make even the most rotten day taste better."

"Thanks. It did." And I meant it. At least for a bit, the sweet *atol* had driven away everything else.

"Good." Walter thumped me on the back. "I'm going back to bed now. See you later."

"'Night."

Walter didn't need to watch *Can You Cut It?* to know what had happened. I'd told him—him and everyone else in town who mattered to me. It was hard at first, but the more times I said it out loud, the easier it got, especially because, like Dad, a lot of people shared their own stories about times they'd messed up. None of them had their stories shown on television to millions of people, but still, it helped.

The worst had been telling Josh and Jeanine. I told them and Zoe on the way back to Petersville after the finals. Zoe didn't seem to get it—or maybe she did and just didn't understand why it was a big deal, as someone who looks at everyone's cards during Go Fish and moves up her piece to the Lollipop Woods in Candy Land when no one's looking. But Josh and Jeanine, they got it, and even though they never said it, I knew they couldn't believe what I'd done.

That's what crushed me: they just couldn't believe it.

Jeanine kept asking questions about how much I'd actually

remembered from Terrence's email, like she was trying to prove that I hadn't even really cheated, and it would have been so easy just to let her, but I couldn't get past this by going backward.

Then there was Winnie. In her opinion, I'd made something about nothing, and then I'd thrown that something—$100,000 of it—in the trash instead of using it to solve our doughnut supply problem. For weeks afterward, every time she saw me, she'd yell, "You never heard 'finders keepers, losers weepers'?" She'd only stopped when Josh and I proved to her that our doughnut collective was starting to work.

I flipped on the lights in The Doughnut Stop, then turned on the computer.

My Doughnut Stop email inbox was brimming with new mail. Big surprise.

I took a deep breath, held it, then clicked.

To: DoughnutBoy@TheDoughnutStop.com
From: Betsy@BetsysMarket.com
Subject: Order

Tris,
    Can we change that order to 20 mocha cream,

same numbers on the others? The mocha was a big hit, and I'm guessing hearing you talk about how you came up with it on *Can You Cut It?* last night will make it an even bigger one.

Thx,

B

I hated to think about Betsy sitting in her living room with her family eating popcorn watching me talk about how I'd cheated. Luckily, what Betsy cared about more than anything else was her store, so she was going to buy from us even if she thought I was a horrible person.

I wrote her back that we'd adjust her order, noted the change on our order sheet, and opened the next email.

To: DoughnutBoy@TheDoughnutStop.com
From: KLT45@imail.com
Re: Can You Cut It?

I could tell from episode 1 you thought you were better than everybody else but now we all know you're just a FRAUD.

I quickly hit Trash, then froze. The *atole* magic was gone.

At least this was an email and not a comment on the website that the whole world could see. Still, way more people watched *Can You Cut It?* last night than ever looked at our website, and they'd all heard me say what I'd done. And this is what they thought, that I was a fraud. It didn't matter that I'd tried to make it right.

I selected the page of emails, all from addresses I didn't recognize, then hovered over the trash.

Could I erase all these emails without reading them? Maybe I deserved to read them?

Click.

To: DoughnutBoy@TheDoughnutStop.com
From: JudyPz221@netspeed.com
Subject: Recipe?

Can you please send me the recipe for your mocha cream?
   Thanks,
   Judy Pitzer
   Omaha, Nebraska

I exhaled. That wasn't scary. Maybe there were other emails like that one.

Click.

CHEATER. CHEATER. CHEATER. CHEATER...

Not that one. I dumped it in the trash, then clicked open the next one.

To: DoughnutBoy@TheDoughnutStop.com
From: KTB33@NapierPrep.com
Subject: Just saying

איך נאָר האָבן איין זאַך צו זאָגן צו איר: איך קען נאָך ענגשאַפּט איר
אין אַלץ אַחוץ באַקינג און באַקומען סטאַק אין עלאַוויטערז 🙂
אָפּרוען מיט אייער קאַפּקייק רעצעפּט און אַלע איז פארגעבן

I stared at the screen. I recognized the symbols as Hebrew. Did they show *Can You Cut It?* in Israel? And why was the subject line in English?

Then it came to me, the last time I saw Hebrew letters.

I copied the email text, then opened a new window, and went to Google Translate. In the first box, I selected Yiddish, in the second box, English. Then I pasted the Hebrew into the Yiddish box and held my breath while *"translating..."* flashed on the screen.

A few moments later, this popped up in the English box:

I just have one thing to say to you:

I could still crush you at everything except baking and getting stuck in elevators. 😊

Respond with your cupcake recipe and all is forgiven.

I laughed. On a day I was sure there would be nothing to laugh about, I laughed.

If anybody had a right to be sending me scary email, it was Keya, and all she wanted was a cupcake recipe.

I hit Reply.

To: KTB33@NapierPrep.com
From: DoughnutBoy@TheDoughnutStop.com
Subject: Re: Just saying

Keya,

Thanks for clearing that up. Will send cupcake recipe soon. Reply with one for butter tea?

Any interest in Skype baking lessons? My rates are reasonable. Just kidding. I owe you.

Tris

After I hit Send, I went through the rest of my inbox.

I'm not going to lie. There was a bunch of hate mail, but I just dumped it right in the trash and didn't think about it again.

Getting the email from Keya had made me realize something. Keya knew me, maybe not like Josh or Jeanine, but she did know me; those other people, the ones who sent the hate mail, didn't. They'd never even met me. Why would I listen to someone who didn't even know me? They were writing to some kid they'd watched on TV, and that kid was just what they saw, not who I was. I knew what I'd done was wrong and how to fix it. I didn't need them for that or anything else.

When I was done with all the mail, I started working on the doughnut schedule, pairing our new dairy collective workers with different orders. I'd been at it only a short time when Jeanine and Zoe came in. Jeanine's eyes were red and Zoe was holding her hand.

"What happened?"

"She's not going to the Oval House. She's sad," Zoe said.

"It's the White *House*. The Oval *Office*," Jeanine said between whimpers. "And I'm not getting to see either."

"You didn't get the scholarship, huh?" I said.

"I...I...I missed the deadline!" Jeanine wailed.

"Wanna hear a duck-duck joke?" Zoe asked.

312

I couldn't believe it. Jeanine had never missed anything in her life. "But how?"

"I don't know," she said. "I guess it was because I was busy, helping Dad with the paper and writing articles. And then when we were in the city, we were out there every day with our signs, trying to get people to listen to our Petersville pitch."

"You missed the deadline for your essay about making a difference because you were too busy making a difference?"

"Not funny."

I went into the office and unpinned the "Twenty-Four Hours in Petersville" *New York Times Travel* article from the wall. By chance, one of the many, many people whose paths Jeanine had blocked on their way to work and held hostage while she did her whole Petersville spiel turned out to be a journalist.

I put the article on the table in front of her. "You did this. That's making a difference."

"I know," she sniffed.

"That's real."

"I know."

"So, that's more important, right? Than a trip to the White House."

"No." She shrugged. "Maybe."

Just then, through the window, I saw a large truck pull slowly into the parking lot. "Did you guys come with Dad?"

"And Mom. They're in the cages." Jeanine wasn't a fan of the shipping containers and refused to call them cottages. "He got his first reservation so he's all, you know…" She jiggled her hands in the air. "Yay."

I went outside.

Josh was just riding up on his bike. "Hey."

"Hey."

The truck came to a stop and made a sound like it was exhaling.

"'Devlin Pack and Ship,'" Josh read off the side. "Your dad get another container?"

"I don't think so."

Two guys wearing matching purple *DPS* shirts and baseball hats climbed out of the cab of the truck.

"Can we help you?" I called.

One of the guys walked over. Pretty sure his name was Otto since that's what was stitched on his shirt pocket. "We're looking for a…" he read off an iPad, "Tris Levin."

Josh and I looked at each other. Hate package?

"Uh, that's me."

Otto squinted at me. "You got I.D.?"

"I'm twelve."

Otto called over his shoulder, "Duke, no I.D.!"

Duke had the back of the truck open now and was lowering a platform with a crate the size of our station wagon to the ground. "Eh, he looks like a Tris."

"Do you know how stupid that sounds?" Otto said.

"Sign says 'The Doughnut Stop,' don't it?" Duke said.

"But maybe this isn't the right 'Doughnut Stop?' Ever think of that, Einstein?"

"I'm pretty sure this is the only one, at least in Petersville," I said.

"We had a real mess once with an Olive Garden delivery." Otto whistled. "A real mess."

"How many times I got to tell you? She gave me the wrong zip code," Duke yelled. "You gonna help me get the dollies under this or what?"

"Um, I didn't order anything this, you know, big. I think it might be a mistake."

"Are you Tris Levin?"

"Yeah but—"

"Is this The Doughnut Stop?"

"Yeah but—"

"And are we in Petersville, New York, 125156?"

"We are."

"Then no mistake." He handed me a stylus and pointed to his iPad. "Sign here."

"I think I should find out what it is first."

"Oh, yeah, there's a note," Otto said. "Duke! Get the kid the note!"

Duke ripped something off the side of the crate and brought me a clear plastic envelope.

I unzipped the envelope and pulled out a typewritten letter:

Mr. Levin,

Funny story:

I was driving through Crellin about a month ago and stopped at a small market. To tell you the truth, I needed to use the bathroom. The woman at the register was kind and directed me to the facilities without insisting that I buy something, but it didn't seem right not to. So on my way out, I looked for a small item to purchase.

I'd skipped lunch so the platter of baked goods on the counter caught my eye. None looked particularly appealing with one exception: a lone, sugar-covered, hole-less doughnut. I asked the woman what was inside. "Butterscotch cream," she said. This meant nothing to me. I've been in this country for many years now, but I'd never even heard this word, butterscotch. The woman said it tasted a bit like caramel, which I like very much, so I decided to take a chance. I assumed I'd take a bite and throw the rest in the trash.

I was surprised when the woman handed me the doughnut wrapped in a napkin, no bag, as if she knew that I'd want to eat it right then and there, and to my surprise, she was right. The second I held it in my hand, I felt compelled to take a bite, something about the weight and the smell demanded that it be eaten that very second.

It was the best doughnut I'd ever tasted, and before I knew it, I'd eaten the whole thing standing right there at the counter.

"Good, right? They're from The Doughnut Stop in Petersville," the woman said. "We order as many as we can, and we always sell out. We'd probably be able to sell three times as many, but they're small batch, you know."

An amazing product made right here in upstate

New York that keeps selling out? I had to learn more. Right then, I sent an email to my assistant back at the office asking him to get me all the information he could on The Doughnut Stop.

By the time I got back to my desk, my assistant was waiting for me with a stack of research and print-outs of two emails—the one you had sent me about investing in The Doughnut Stop and the one Majani sent you declining the opportunity. Quite by accident, my assistant had run a search for "The Doughnut Stop" on our internal server and the emails had popped up.

I must confess, I receive too many emails to review them all. I leave it to people I trust to decide which emails make it to my desk. In the case of yours, a mistake was made. In their defense, they'd never tasted the doughnuts.

I am hoping to rectify this mistake now. Please excuse the delay. I look forward to hearing from you soon.

Your friend,
Alhaadi Okello

"So?" Duke said. "What is it?"

"No way!" Josh had been reading over my shoulder and was jumping up and down.

I couldn't believe it. The Tea King had bought us a Donut Robot?

We'd been doing much better with our doughnut collective than we'd done without it, but it was messy and complicated, and we still couldn't meet demand. But the Donut Robot would change all that. We could give people jobs to run it around the clock, to make all different flavors. We could hire more drivers to deliver doughnuts all over the area.

"Come on," Otto said. "We got it all the way here. You're not going to tell us what's inside."

"A robot," I said.

"Oh, okay. Sure. Somebody sent you a robot the size of a jeep. And you didn't even know it was coming." Duke rolled his eyes.

"Really," I said.

"Oh, yeah?" Otto said. "What's it do then, this robot? Like clean your house and drive your car?"

"Massage your feet?" Duke laughed.

"It keeps towns from disappearing," I said.

Duke and Otto cracked up, but I didn't care, because I knew it would—or we would with the robot's help, and everyone else's too. Petersville would never become a D-word.

So come taste The Petersville Experience yourself! Feel the rush you can only get from filling your own life-changing doughnut with any one of five mind-blowing creams. Sample the Pop Shop's mystery flavor popcorn. Make your own mozzarella at the Stinky Cheese Farm Store. Watch the *Wizard of Oz* on a big screen while you get your hair cut in the style of your favorite character and make a yellow-brick road quilt. Have an award-winning chicken potpie dinner at The Station House, then spend the night in an old shipping container, and wake up to a breakfast of *atole* and pupusas. Who knows? Maybe we'll even have a five-yolk egg to show you by then. Either way, we're not going anywhere. I promise.

KEYA'S SPICED BUTTER TEA

Ingredients

2 teabags of Rooibos, English Breakfast, or Earl Grey

½ tsp cloves

½ tsp cardamom

½ tsp cinnamon

¼ tsp turmeric

¼ tsp ground ginger

½ cup of coconut milk*

1 ½ tbsp unsalted butter (the better the butter, the better the taste; try grass-fed)

brown sugar

sea salt

Directions

1. Pour 4 cups of water into a saucepan and put on medium heat. Add spices to the water and stir until simmering.

2. Put heat on low. Add tea bags for 2–4 minutes.

3. Remove bags.

4. Add coconut milk and butter, gently stirring as the butter melts.

5. Turn off heat. Then sweeten with brown sugar to taste (1–2 tbsps).

6. Drop in pinch of sea salt and stir.

7. Pour into mugs and enjoy!

*Fun fact: under the rules of One-Ingredient Masterpiece, the coconut milk is the one ingredient that counted!

ONE-INGREDIENT CHOCOLATE MOUSSE

Ingredients

4 ounces of good quality semi-sweet chocolate

3 ounces of water

Directions

1. Fill a large mixing bowl with ice cubes and nestle a smaller mixing bowl in ice.

2. Melt chocolate with the water on the stove on low.

3. When chocolate is smooth and combined with water, pour into the smaller mixing bowl in the ice, and whisk by hand or with a hand mixer continuously until mixture thickens (approximately 3–5 minutes).

4. If mixture doesn't want to mousse up, melt a little more chocolate, add to the mixture, and whisk again. If mixture thickens too much, you can re-melt and start again.

5. Once mixture thickens, spoon immediately into serving bowls.

6. For extra *wow*, drizzle with olive oil and sprinkle with sea salt. Gobble up!

PEEKABOO MOCHA CREAM CUPCAKES

Makes 12 cupcakes

Ingredients

Cupcakes:

1½ cups all-purpose flour

1 tsp baking powder

½ tsp salt

3 eggs

1 stick unsalted butter (melted)

1 cup sugar

1 tbsp vanilla

¾ cup buttermilk

Mocha Cream:

1 cup unsalted butter (softened)

3½ cups of powdered sugar (sifted or whisked to remove clumps)

¼ cup of heavy cream

¼ cup of decaf espresso (room temperature)

2 tbsp cocoa powder

ground nutmeg

Cupcake Directions:

1. Preheat oven to 350 degrees.
2. Put cupcake liners in the cupcake tins.
3. Whisk together flour, salt, and baking powder.
4. Crack eggs into a small bowl and beat lightly.
5. Mix melted butter and sugar in a stand mixer on medium until thick. Pour in eggs and vanilla. Continue mixing until combined.
6. Add a third of the flour mixture, a third of the buttermilk, then mix until just combined.
7. Repeat two more times until all flour and buttermilk is combined.
8. Fill lined cupcake tins ⅔ full.
9. Bake for approximately 15–20 minutes. Cupcakes are done when a toothpick comes out clean.
10. Cool before frosting.

Mocha Cream Instructions:

1. Cut butter into pieces, then cream in a mixer.
2. Add powdered sugar in batches, mixing until thick.
3. Combine heavy cream, espresso, pinch of nutmeg, and cocoa powder.
4. Add in batches to the frosting, mixing and tasting after each addition.

5. Stop when you reach your perfect mocha flavor. You may not use all the liquid.
6. If frosting seems like it's getting runny, add a bit more powdered sugar to thicken.

Filling/Frosting Instructions:
1. Put sunburst tip on pastry bag.
2. Fill bag with cream.
3. Push tip into the center of the top of cupcake.
4. Fill with cream just until the top of the cake begins to pull apart, then spiral cream over the hole and the top of the cupcake. Enjoy!

ACKNOWLEDGMENTS

I had many years to finish *The Doughnut Fix*. *The Doughnut King* was a very different experience. I had a deadline, and I was terrified. What if the words didn't come when I needed them? Readers, teachers, librarians, booksellers, your support for *The Doughnut Fix* and your response to these characters drove my doubts away and inspired me every day I sat down to write. This book is for, and because of, you.

I am grateful to my editor Annie Berger for her unwavering belief in me and for her incredible editorial letter on the roughest of rough drafts. Thank you to everyone at Sourcebooks, in particular to Lauren Dombrowski and Sarah Kasman, and to Nina Goffi for another gorgeous cover. Thank you to my agent Carrie Hannigan everyone at HSG, and publicist Deb Shapiro for their tremendous advice and support.

My Vermont College of Fine Arts family, the Writers of the Lost Arc, and Cynthia Leitich Smith, your support keeps me afloat. Thank you in particular to Tim Wynne-Jones, Varian Johnson, and David Gill for your guidance on the early pages of this book.

To friends and family who sent photos of their kids reading the first book, bought copies for everyone they knew, gave them out as party favors, attended book launches, arranged school visits, hosted book parties, became book promotion machines (Abby Nachtomi Feldman!), you are the human equivalent of life-changing chocolate cream doughnuts.

A huge thank-you to Dad, Will, Crystal, Pascale, Judy, Alan, Ben, Lizzie, and especially Sam and Teddy for their enthusiastic support.

And finally, the biggest thanks of all goes to the home team, and not just because you put up with me day in and day out, but because none of this would be possible without you. Eddie, wonder twin powers activate forever and ever! Toby, Leo, and Sylvie, you are my story whisperers, my champions, and my most miraculous creations.

ABOUT THE AUTHOR

Jessie Janowitz grew up in New York City and is still living there with her husband and three children, all of whom love doughnuts as much as she does.